Grave Tales: Discovering the Lives of Beth Israel

The Grave Whisperer

Angeline Gallant

Published by Angeline Gallant, 2024.

While every precaution has been taken in the preparation of this book, the publisher assumes no responsibility for errors or omissions, or for damages resulting from the use of the information contained herein.

GRAVE TALES: DISCOVERING THE LIVES OF BETH ISRAEL

First edition. October 29, 2024.

Copyright © 2024 Angeline Gallant.

ISBN: 979-8227822024

Written by Angeline Gallant.

Also by Angeline Gallant

A Dragon's Diary
Dreaming of Dragons

Calling Her Heart
Whisper of the Heart
No Turning Back
Forsake Me Not
Hear My Cry

FORGET ME NOT
Victoria, Ontario's Babies 1894 - 1895

GENERATIONS OF THE VOLGA
A Family's Legacy

Guardian of the Heart
Fallen Petals

Keeper Of Secrets
A Lady's Secret

Kingston's Love Chronicles
Springtime Promises

Midnight's Awakening
Heart of the Storm
Walking Through The Storm
Walking Through The Storm
Heart of the Storm

Secrets of the Underworld
Deklan's Dragons

Tell My Story Collection
Tell My Story: Germany 1851
Tell My Story: England 1852
Whispers From The Garrison Church

The Dervock Legacy
Echoes of Dervock

The Grave Whisperer
Cataraqui United Church Cemetery
Wedding Bells in Kingston, Ontario, Canada 1923
St. Paul's Anglican Churchyard Kingston, Ontario, Canada A-B
St. Paul's Anglican Churchyard, Kingston, Ontario, Canada C - D
St. Paul's Anglican Churchyard, Kingston, Ontario, Canada G - H
St. Paul's Anglican Churchyard, Kingston, Ontario, Canada J - N
St. Paul's Anglican Churchyard, Kingston, Ontario, Canada O - R
St. Paul's Anglican Churchyard, Kingston, Ontario, Canada S - T
St. Paul's Anglican Churchyard, Kingston, Ontario T - Z
Small Graveyards & Burial Grounds: Kingston, Ontario, Canada
Cataraqui United Church Cemetery 1
Cataraqui United Church Cemetery 2
Cataraqui United Church Cemetary 3
Cataraqui United Church Cemetery 4
Cataraqui United Church Cemetery 5
Beth Israel Cemetery
Cataraqui United Church Cemetery 6
Beneath the Surface: Echoes from Beth Israel Cemetery
Grave Tales: Discovering the Lives of Beth Israel

The Timeless Veil
Eternal Devotion

The Wolf Whisperer Series
Journey of the Heart
Cry of a Warrior
Wolf Whisperer volumes 1 & 2

Endless White
The Wolf Whisperer volumes 1 & 2

Timeless
The Time Keeper's Sanctuary

Timeless Whispers of Dervock Saga
Secrets of Dervock

Standalone
Winds of Change vol 1-3

Table of Contents

Aaron Samuel Kizell[1]

Aaron was born in Ontario, Canada on August 3, 1919. With deep Lithuanian Jewish roots, his birth marked a continuation of family heritage in a world still finding its way after the upheaval of World War I. Canada was slowly recovering from the war, mourning its lost soldiers while celebrating the return of those who survived.

For Jewish families with ties to Eastern Europe, like Aaron's, this was a time of significant change. Lithuania had only recently declared its independence from Russia in 1918, allowing many Lithuanian Jews, especially those in Canada, to hope for stability and peace for their homeland after centuries of turmoil. Yet, as much as Canada offered a new beginning, echoes of the old country resonated in communities, synagogues, and homes. Yiddish was often spoken alongside English, and traditions were upheld as a bridge between the worlds they left and the lives they were building.

Aaron's early years would have been surrounded by stories of resilience, of family members who'd crossed oceans for the promise of a better life, and of preserving identity amidst the Canadian melting pot. He was born into an era where the threads of history and ancestry were woven tightly, a gift he inherited and carried forward.

AT JUST TWO YEARS OLD, little Aaron Samuel became a big brother when his sister, Doris, was born in the quiet town of Killaloe, Ontario, in October of 1921. The small rural community nestled in the Ottawa Valley was a close-knit place, where neighbors knew one another, and families supported each other through the challenges of the early 20th century.

The world that Doris entered was one still impacted by the aftermath of the Great War, but it was also an era of growth and promise. In homes like theirs, the old traditions and the Yiddish language of their Lithuanian Jewish heritage wove seamlessly with their new Canadian lives. The Kizell family, like so many others in rural Ontario, likely shared an enduring hope for their children's futures, along with a determination to build a strong foundation of faith, family, and community.

BY THE TIME AARON TURNED four, he was already a seasoned big brother, ready to welcome another sibling into the family. On a crisp January day in 1924, little Raymond Harold was born, adding yet another thread to the rich tapestry of the Kizell family's story. In those early years, the Kizell children would have experienced a childhood marked by simple joys and the rhythms of small-town life.

In 1924, rural Ontario was still in the age of horse-drawn carriages and wood-burning stoves, where winter nights meant gathering close to keep warm and listening to family stories passed down from their Lithuanian roots. For Jewish families like the Kizells, this was a time of balancing heritage and new beginnings. Through family celebrations, observances, and language, the children would have felt both the strength of their Jewish identity and the dreams of their parents to create a meaningful life in Canada.

AT THE AGE OF FIVE, Aaron's world grew a little bigger with the arrival of his sister, Greta, born on July 11, 1925. Now, with three younger siblings, the Kizell household must have been a lively place, filled with laughter, squabbles, and the warmth that only a bustling family can bring.

The 1920s in Ontario was a time of change and adaptation for many Jewish families like the Kizells. For the children, this often meant learning about Jewish traditions at home while navigating the Canadian landscape outside. In this environment, Aaron might have begun taking on the role of a protector, feeling a special responsibility for his growing family. In those days, he likely accompanied his parents to the local synagogue, where the children would see their community's values come to life—strength, resilience, and the importance of family.

———————————

IN 1931, AARON WAS an 11-year-old boy growing up in Ottawa, living with his family at 333 Besserer Avenue. At the time, Ottawa was a growing city, and neighborhoods like his were filled with families adapting to new surroundings, some just beginning to find their footing in a Canadian way of life.

That year's census recorded Aaron as Irish—a curious note given his Lithuanian Jewish heritage. This surprising detail hints at the era's complexities where ethnicities and identities were sometimes misrepresented. For a young Jewish boy like Aaron, these subtleties may have added another layer to the challenges of balancing cultural identity with daily life in Canada.

Still, 1931 was a vibrant year for Ottawa's Jewish community. Aaron and his family likely participated in local Jewish traditions and community events, finding comfort in shared practices while embracing their new Canadian roots. It was a childhood that, in small yet meaningful ways, was helping to shape the identity of a young boy whose life would be woven into the rich tapestry of Canadian Jewish history.

AARON WENT ON TO MARRY Birdie Rae Cramer, a fellow member of the Jewish community, whose shared heritage and values deepened their bond. Together, they built a life rooted in tradition, mutual respect, and an enduring connection to their cultural heritage. In those years, Jewish families in Canada often found strength and comfort in marriage partnerships that preserved customs, stories, and shared values—a continuity that Aaron and Birdie would have treasured in a world that was rapidly changing around them.

Their marriage symbolized not just the union of two people, but the blending of two families with deep histories, traditions, and experiences. Together, they celebrated Jewish festivals, upheld sacred customs, and perhaps even shared stories of their ancestors' journeys from Eastern Europe to Canada—a legacy they would pass down to future generations. Birdie's support, warmth, and shared understanding of their background would have enriched Aaron's life as they carved out a meaningful life together, navigating challenges and joys as partners and as a family.

AT 37, AARON WITNESSED a historic milestone with the launch of Sputnik in 1957, an event that marked the beginning of the Space Age and dramatically shifted global perspectives. The launch of the Soviet satellite sparked a newfound curiosity about space exploration and captured the world's imagination, with many Canadians eagerly following each development in the race beyond Earth's boundaries.

For Aaron, living through such a revolutionary time would have meant seeing the world transform in unimaginable ways. The pace of technological change brought a mix of wonder and uncertainty, as new inventions and discoveries reshaped daily life. In Jewish communities across Canada, the conversation around Sputnik likely intertwined with discussions about tradition, adaptation, and the impact of progress. As a husband, brother, and member of his community, Aaron would have experienced this era not just as an individual but as part of a wider community adjusting to a rapidly evolving world while preserving the values that anchored them.

AT 41, AARON SAW ANOTHER breathtaking leap in human achievement as Yuri Gagarin, the Russian astronaut, became the first human to orbit the Earth in 1961. This incredible feat represented a new era of exploration and innovation, one that touched people from all walks of life, even thousands of miles away in Ontario.

For Aaron and those around him, this moment may have brought a sense of awe and possibility, along with the weight of Cold War tensions felt worldwide. People in Canada and across the globe were captivated by the daring and bravery of space exploration, as well as the profound questions it raised about humanity's future and place in the universe. This year also sparked conversations in Jewish and other communities alike about how these profound advances in technology and human potential aligned with spiritual beliefs and cultural values.

In those years, community gatherings, like those Aaron may have attended, would have been rich with debate over these advances, blending tradition with curiosity about what lay beyond the stars.

WHEN AARON WAS 50, he faced the profound loss of his father, Archibald, who passed away on August 5, 1969, in Kingston, Ontario. Losing a parent at any age is a profound milestone, and for Aaron, it likely marked a reflective chapter in his life, as he may have taken stock of his own journey while honoring his father's memory. Archibald's passing would have drawn the family together in a time of collective remembrance, reflecting on the legacy and values he left behind.

This year was also a time of transformation across Canada and the world. Just a month earlier, humankind took its first steps on the moon—a breathtaking feat that forever altered humanity's view of itself and its capabilities. For Aaron, this era of human accomplishment might have brought bittersweet feelings, contrasting the heights of achievement with the personal depths of loss.

AT 62, AARON WITNESSED a defining moment in Canadian history: the passing of the Canada Act in 1982. This landmark legislation, signed by Queen Elizabeth II, officially granted Canada full sovereignty, allowing it to amend its own constitution without British approval. For Canadians, particularly those with deep roots in the country like Aaron, this was a powerful affirmation of national identity and independence. It was a moment that spoke to generations of change, growth, and the evolution of a country that had long been forging its own path.

By this stage in life, Aaron had likely developed a strong sense of what Canada meant to him and his family. With his own Lithuanian Jewish heritage, he would have understood the value of cultural identity and resilience. This significant year may have stirred reflections on how Canada had shaped his life and the lives of his children, a nation now fully its own, rich in diversity, history, and freedom.

AT 64, AARON FACED a profound loss when his beloved wife, Birdie Rae, passed away on February 5, 1984, in Kingston, Ontario. Birdie, a cherished partner and fellow Jew, had been by his side through the joys and challenges of life, and her absence left a significant void.

Birdie's passing marked a poignant chapter in Aaron's life, as they had built a family together, weaving their stories into the fabric of their community. Memories of their life together would have filled his heart—her laughter, their shared dreams, and the love they nurtured for their children and grandchildren.

In the years following Birdie's death, Aaron likely found solace in the connections they had forged, the family they had raised, and the shared history that had been their life. This loss would have reminded him of the fragility of life and the importance of cherishing each moment with loved ones, pushing him to honor Birdie's memory in any way he could, perhaps by sharing stories of their life together with their children or involving himself more deeply in their community.

AT THE AGE OF 67, AARON Samuel Kizell passed away in Kingston, Ontario, in 1987. His death marked the end of a life filled with rich experiences, family ties, and a deep connection to his Jewish heritage. Having faced the loss of his wife, Birdie, and the passage of time, Aaron's final years likely held reflections on his life's journey and the legacy he would leave behind.

Aaron was laid to rest in Beth Israel Cemetery, a sacred space that serves as a testament to the lives and stories of the Jewish community in Kingston. There, beneath the serene landscape, his family and friends could visit, honoring the man who had devoted his life to his loved ones and community.

As generations came to remember him, they would gather to share stories of Aaron's kindness, his resilience, and the values he instilled in them. His life would continue to echo through the memories of those he touched, solidifying his place in the hearts of his family, now united in their shared history and heritage.

Birdie Rae (Cramer) Kizell[2]

Birdie Rae Cramer was born in 1926, a year marked by both optimism and significant global challenges. The world was still reeling from the effects of World War I, and the roaring twenties were in full swing, particularly in North America. It was a time of cultural change, economic prosperity, and social transformation.

In the United States, the economy was booming, and cities were filled with jazz music, flapper fashion, and a spirit of celebration. However, this era of excess was also leading to underlying economic disparities that would soon culminate in the Great Depression. The stock market was on the rise, and many families were beginning to enjoy a higher standard of living, with advancements in technology and industry contributing to a new consumer culture.

In Canada, Birdie's birthplace would have reflected similar cultural influences, as well as the ongoing evolution of Canadian society. The 1920s were characterized by a strong sense of national identity, and the Jewish community, including Birdie's family, was growing and becoming more integrated into Canadian life while maintaining their rich cultural traditions.

As a Jewish girl born in this era, Birdie would have been surrounded by a close-knit community, one that placed a strong emphasis on family, education, and cultural values. The events of the time, along with the Jewish diaspora's experiences, would shape her identity and the values she carried into her adult life.

Birdie Rae's early years were set against a backdrop of both excitement and uncertainty, laying the foundation for a life that would be intertwined with her husband Aaron and their family in Kingston, Ontario.

BIRDIE RAE CRAMER WAS just six years old when Joseph Stalin began imposing his reign of terror in the Soviet Union. This period, marked by widespread repression, purges, and famines, had profound implications not only for those living in Russia but also for Jewish communities worldwide, including those in Canada.

Although Birdie was living in Kingston, Ontario, far from the immediate horrors of Stalin's policies, the ripple effects were felt globally. Families of Jewish heritage, including Birdie's own, were acutely aware of the struggles faced by their brethren in Eastern Europe. Many were concerned for relatives still living in regions impacted by oppressive regimes, and news of the purges and famines often reached them through community networks.

In Kingston, the Jewish community likely rallied together during this tumultuous time, providing support and solidarity to one another. Synagogues would have served as both spiritual havens and community centers, where families gathered to pray and share news.

Birdie's childhood would have been influenced by stories of resilience and survival that were common among immigrant families. The memory of oppression likely instilled in her a strong sense of identity and pride in her Jewish heritage, along with a desire to uphold family traditions and values.

This was a formative time for Birdie, as she navigated her early years with the knowledge that her community was connected to a broader narrative of struggle and hope. The terror inflicted by Stalin served as a reminder of the importance of unity, faith, and the preservation of culture, elements that would become integral parts of Birdie's life as she grew into adulthood.

———

BIRDIE RAE CRAMER WAS 31 years old when the Soviet Union launched Sputnik 1 on October 4, 1957, marking a significant milestone in space exploration and igniting the Space Race between the United States and the Soviet Union. The launch of the world's first artificial satellite captured global attention and stirred a wave of excitement and anxiety across nations, including Canada.

Living in Kingston, Ontario, Birdie would have experienced the thrill of this new technological advancement and the implications it carried for the future. As the news spread, discussions in households, schools, and communities likely revolved around the satellite's potential to change life on Earth. The sound of Sputnik's beeping signal as it orbited the planet became a symbol of the era, sparking both wonder and concern about the capabilities of science and technology, and the competition between superpowers.

As a Jewish woman with a background rooted in resilience, Birdie might have viewed the launch of Sputnik as both an opportunity and a challenge. The excitement of scientific progress likely resonated with her values of perseverance and education, encouraging her to instill similar ideals in her children and community.

Additionally, the Space Race was intertwined with Cold War politics, which would have had a ripple effect on Canadian society. Birdie's awareness of global affairs may have prompted her to engage in conversations about national security, the importance of education in science and technology, and the role of Canada in international relations.

For Birdie, the launch of Sputnik could have served as a reminder of the rapid changes happening in the world around her, spurring her interest in advancements that could impact her family and community. The excitement of space exploration, along with the underlying tensions of the Cold War, shaped the backdrop of her early 30s, marking a time of profound transformation and inspiration for generations to come.

————

BIRDIE RAE CRAMER WAS 56 years old when audio CDs were introduced to the market in 1982, revolutionizing the way people listened to music and consumed audio content. This technological advancement marked a significant shift from vinyl records and cassette tapes to a more compact, high-quality digital format, paving the way for the future of music distribution.

Living in Kingston, Ontario, Birdie likely experienced the excitement surrounding this innovation firsthand. The arrival of CDs brought a sense of modernity and convenience, enabling her to enjoy her favorite music with enhanced sound clarity. She may have found joy in exploring new music, curating her collection, and perhaps introducing her children to a broader array of artists and genres.

The introduction of CDs also coincided with a cultural shift in the early 1980s, characterized by vibrant music scenes, including the rise of pop, rock, and new wave. Birdie might have embraced this era of musical exploration, attending concerts or sharing the experience of music with family and friends. The transition from analog to digital would have sparked conversations about the evolving landscape of the music industry and the changing ways people connected with art and entertainment.

As a Jewish woman who valued community and family, Birdie might have used music as a means to bring loved ones together. Family gatherings could have featured sing-alongs or shared listening sessions, where stories of her past intertwined with the melodies of contemporary artists. The emotional power of music, now available on a small disc, likely resonated deeply with her, creating cherished memories and fostering connections.

In addition to music, the introduction of CDs also represented the broader technological advancements of the 1980s, impacting everything from personal computing to entertainment. Birdie's adaptability and openness to new ideas would have allowed her to embrace these changes, encouraging her family to appreciate the benefits of modern technology while also cherishing the traditions that shaped their Jewish heritage.

For Birdie, the advent of audio CDs was not just a technological innovation but a gateway to new experiences, connections, and memories that she would treasure for years to come.

BIRDIE RAE CRAMER PASSED away in Kingston, Ontario, on February 5, 1984, at the age of 58, leaving behind a legacy woven into the fabric of her family and community. Her passing marked the end of a vibrant life that had witnessed profound changes in society, culture, and technology.

In her later years, Birdie likely reflected on the joys and challenges she faced throughout her life, from her childhood during the tumultuous years of Stalin's reign to her adult experiences in a rapidly changing world. She may have been deeply rooted in her Jewish faith and heritage, sharing traditions and values with her family, creating a nurturing environment for her children, and instilling in them the importance of community and connection.

Her family would remember her as a loving mother and grandmother who valued relationships, celebrated life's milestones, and supported her loved ones through thick and thin. Birdie's home might have been a gathering place for family celebrations, where laughter filled the air, and the warmth of togetherness was palpable.

As someone who experienced significant historical events, Birdie's life mirrored the resilience of her generation. She navigated the ups and downs of life with grace, facing the realities of the world while remaining optimistic about the future. Her story is a testament to the strength of family bonds and the enduring spirit of those who came before us.

Birdie Rae Cramer's burial in Beth Israel Cemetery is a poignant reminder of her life and the impact she had on those around her. The gravestone may serve as a tribute to her contributions, not just as a member of her family but as a cherished member of the Kingston community. Those who visit her resting place might pause to reflect on her journey, the challenges she overcame, and the love she shared.

Though Birdie is no longer physically present, her spirit lives on through the stories her family shares, the traditions she established, and the values she instilled in those who continue to honor her memory. In remembering Birdie Rae Cramer, we celebrate a life rich with experiences, resilience, and love—a life that remains an integral part of the tapestry of history in Kingston, Ontario.

Joan Rita (Cowan) Kizell[3]

———

J oan was born in 1933, a year marked by significant global challenges and changes. The Great Depression was still affecting economies worldwide, and many families faced financial hardships and uncertainty. In North America, unemployment rates were high, and communities were struggling to find stability amidst the economic turmoil.

For Jewish families like Joan's, life was filled with both hope and trepidation. Many Jewish communities sought refuge in countries like Canada and the United States, hoping to escape social and economic challenges.

Despite these difficulties, the early 1930s also witnessed cultural developments. The arts flourished in various forms, with music, literature, and film providing an escape from the hardships of daily life. In Jewish communities, cultural and religious practices offered solace and a sense of belonging. Families came together for traditional gatherings, celebrating holidays and fostering connections through shared values and customs.

In the United States, the New Deal was implemented by President Franklin D. Roosevelt to revive the economy and provide relief to struggling Americans. These initiatives aimed to support families, create jobs, and stimulate growth, which would eventually help lift the country out of the depths of the Great Depression.

Joan's early years were shaped by these complexities. She may have been surrounded by a close-knit family that emphasized the importance of community, resilience, and faith during challenging times. As she grew, the world around her continued to evolve, setting the stage for significant historical events that would influence her life and the lives of those around her. The trials and triumphs of the 1930s would undoubtedly impact her perspective and experiences as she navigated her own path in a world marked by uncertainty and change.

JOAN WAS 24 YEARS OLD when Sputnik was launched on October 4, 1957, marking a pivotal moment in history. This event was not just significant in the realm of science and technology; it represented the beginning of the Space Age and the U.S.-Soviet space race. The launch of the first artificial satellite ignited a wave of excitement and fear around the world, particularly in the United States, where the public felt a sense of urgency to compete with the Soviet Union in technological advancements.

For Joan, this was a time of exploration and innovation. The launch captured the imagination of a generation, inspiring dreams of space travel and scientific discovery. Many young people in her community looked to the future with optimism, captivated by the possibilities that advancements in technology promised. Education became a priority, as students were encouraged to pursue careers in science, mathematics, and engineering to ensure their nation kept pace with the rapidly advancing world.

As a young Jewish woman in the 1950s, Joan may have also been involved in community activities that sought to foster progress and solidarity. The period was marked by a strong sense of identity and activism among Jewish communities, as they worked to promote social justice and civil rights. Joan's generation played an integral role in shaping the future, balancing the thrill of new discoveries with the pressing social issues of the time.

In her personal life, Joan may have been navigating the challenges of young adulthood, possibly contemplating her career aspirations, forming lasting relationships, or starting a family. The excitement surrounding the launch of Sputnik likely influenced her worldview, instilling a sense of curiosity and a desire to be part of the changes unfolding around her. As she stepped into the future, Joan carried with her the hopes and dreams of a generation eager to explore new frontiers, both in space and in their own lives.

JOAN MARRIED RAYMOND Howard Kizell, further intertwining their lives and legacies. Born into a Jewish family, Raymond likely shared with Joan a rich cultural heritage and values that shaped their upbringing. Their union in a time marked by significant social and technological change would have provided a solid foundation for their shared experiences and aspirations.

As a couple, Joan and Raymond would have navigated the complexities of life in the mid-20th century, dealing with the shifting dynamics of society while also cherishing their cultural identity. They may have participated in community events, Jewish traditions, and celebrations that reinforced their bond and connection to their roots.

Together, they likely raised a family, instilling in their children the importance of their Jewish heritage, as well as the values of resilience and community that defined their upbringing. Their marriage would have been a partnership not only in personal growth but also in facing the challenges and triumphs of their time, creating a shared history that reflected both their individual journeys and their collective aspirations.

Joan and Raymond's life together was likely enriched by mutual support as they navigated the challenges of the changing world around them, including the impacts of the Cold War, technological advancements, and social movements. They would have celebrated milestones and faced adversities hand in hand, crafting a legacy that resonates through their family and community today.

———————

JOAN WAS 49 YEARS OLD when audio CDs were introduced in 1982, heralding a new era in music consumption. This shift marked a departure from traditional vinyl records and cassette tapes, offering a more convenient and higher-quality listening experience. For Joan, the arrival of CDs likely sparked excitement as she explored a vast array of genres and artists, rediscovering her favorite music and discovering new sounds.

The 1980s were a vibrant time for music, with the rise of pop, rock, and new wave, and Joan may have relished the opportunity to enjoy iconic albums that defined the decade. The clarity of sound provided by CDs would have allowed her to appreciate the nuances in music she had loved for years, enhancing her listening experience.

As someone with a rich cultural heritage, the introduction of audio CDs may have inspired Joan to reflect on the role of music in her life and how it connects to her Jewish identity. She could have engaged with the broader cultural shifts of the time, enjoying concerts, discovering new artists, and participating in the vibrant music scene.

The transition to this new format represented not just a technological advancement but also a reminder of the changes and adaptations she had witnessed throughout her life. Joan's appreciation for music may have deepened as she embraced the innovation while holding onto the traditions that shaped her, weaving a rich tapestry of experiences that reflected her journey.

———————

JOAN WAS 56 YEARS OLD when her father, Maurice Cowen, passed away on December 14, 1989. Losing a parent is a profound moment in anyone's life, and for Joan, this loss likely brought a mix of sorrow and reflection. Maurice had been a significant figure in her life, shaping her values and beliefs, particularly in the context of their shared Jewish heritage.

In the late 1980s, society was experiencing significant changes, from advancements in technology to shifts in cultural norms. Joan may have found comfort in the memories of her father's stories and the lessons he imparted, especially as the world around her evolved rapidly. The Jewish community, with its strong traditions and communal ties, would have provided her with support during this difficult time, allowing her to honor her father's legacy in meaningful ways.

As she navigated her grief, Joan might have also been drawn to the comforting rituals of her faith, finding solace in prayer and remembrance. This period could have prompted her to reflect on family history, her father's life experiences, and how they intertwined with her own journey.

Joan's relationship with her father would have influenced her perspectives on life, love, and loss, shaping her as she moved forward into the 1990s, a decade poised to bring new challenges and opportunities. The memories of Maurice would forever remain a part of her, guiding her through the changes that lay ahead.

JOAN WAS 68 YEARS OLD when the tragic events of September 11, 2001, unfolded. The day marked a profound shift in global awareness and security, leaving an indelible mark on society. For Joan, witnessing the aftermath of 9/11 would have stirred a complex mix of emotions, as it did for many—fear, sadness, and a deep sense of vulnerability.

In the wake of the attacks, the world was enveloped in a wave of grief, and the Jewish community, like many others, came together in solidarity. Joan may have found herself reflecting on the importance of community and the resilience that often arises in the face of adversity. As news of the attacks dominated the headlines, conversations in her social circles likely shifted towards issues of safety, tolerance, and the responsibilities of citizenship.

During this time, Joan could have also felt a renewed commitment to her values of compassion and understanding, considering how important it is to build bridges across cultural divides. She might have participated in community gatherings or interfaith dialogues aimed at fostering peace and unity in an increasingly fragmented world.

The events of 9/11 may have led Joan to reflect on her own family's history, the struggles they faced, and the strength that had carried them through. With the lessons of the past in mind, she likely sought to support those around her, emphasizing kindness and empathy in her interactions. As she navigated this new chapter in history, Joan would remain a steadfast presence for her friends and family, embodying the enduring spirit of resilience and hope.

JOAN WAS 69 YEARS OLD when her mother, Eunice Edith (née Breslin), passed away on November 3, 2002. The loss of a parent is a profound moment in anyone's life, and for Joan, this was no exception. Eunice had been a guiding force and a source of strength throughout Joan's life, and losing her marked a significant transition.

As Joan navigated her grief, she would likely have reflected on the rich memories they shared, recalling the lessons Eunice imparted and the love that had always been a constant in their relationship. In Jewish tradition, honoring one's parents is of utmost importance, and Joan may have sought ways to commemorate her mother's legacy. This could have included participating in memorial services, reciting Kaddish, and gathering family and friends to share stories about Eunice, ensuring that her spirit lived on in the hearts of those who loved her.

During this period, Joan might have felt a deeper connection to her roots and heritage, considering how Eunice had influenced her identity. She could have also been prompted to think about her own role as a matriarch within her family, recognizing the importance of passing down traditions, values, and stories to keep her mother's memory alive.

In the years following Eunice's passing, Joan may have become more involved in community activities or charitable efforts, channeling her grief into helping others. She might have also sought to strengthen her relationships with her extended family, understanding the significance of connection during challenging times. As she continued to navigate life without her mother, Joan's resilience and commitment to family and community would have remained unwavering, ensuring that Eunice's love and lessons continued to resonate in her life and the lives of those around her.

JOAN WAS 70 YEARS OLD when her husband, Raymond Harold Kizell, passed away in Kingston, Ontario, on May 31, 2003. Losing a life partner is one of the most heart-wrenching experiences one can endure, and for Joan, this loss would have marked another profound chapter in her life.

Raymond and Joan shared a deep bond, rooted in love and shared experiences. His passing would have left a significant void in her daily life, as they had likely created countless memories together. As she faced this new reality without him, Joan would have navigated the complexities of grief, reflecting on their journey as a couple and cherishing the moments that defined their relationship.

During this time, she might have drawn comfort from their shared history—recalling the laughter, the challenges they overcame, and the love that sustained them through the years. Joan may have also found solace in the Jewish practices that provide structure and comfort in mourning, such as sitting shiva, where family and friends gather to support one another in their shared grief.

As she moved through the mourning process, Joan would have likely relied on her community for support, connecting with friends and family who understood the depth of her loss. This connection might have been particularly important as she navigated the various stages of grief, from sadness to remembrance, and perhaps even to acceptance.

In the wake of Raymond's death, Joan could have considered ways to honor his memory—perhaps by engaging in charitable activities they both cared about or by continuing traditions they had established together. She may have sought to keep his spirit alive by sharing stories about him, ensuring that the legacy of their love continued to resonate within her heart and in the lives of those who knew them both.

Joan's resilience would shine through during this challenging period, as she embraced the memories of her husband while also navigating her own path forward, carrying the lessons and love they shared into the next chapters of her life.

JOAN WAS 77 YEARS OLD when she passed away in Kingston on March 8, 2010. Her passing marked the end of a life rich with experiences, memories, and the indelible mark she left on those who knew her. By this time, Joan had lived through decades of significant historical events, cultural shifts, and personal milestones that shaped her worldview and her relationships.

As her family and friends gathered to remember her, they would have reflected on the many ways Joan had touched their lives. Known for her kindness, compassion, and unwavering support, she likely left behind a legacy of love that resonated deeply with her community.

Her burial in Beth Israel Cemetery would have been a poignant moment, surrounded by the familiar names and faces of her Jewish heritage. This sacred space held not just the memories of those who had come before her, but also the stories and traditions that Joan cherished throughout her life. As her loved ones gathered to pay their respects, they would have shared stories of her strength, resilience, and the laughter that filled her home.

In her final resting place, Joan was reunited with her husband, Raymond, and honored alongside her parents, Maurice and Eunice. Her life, woven into the fabric of her family's history, would continue to inspire future generations. Those who visited her grave would be reminded of her warmth and the countless moments they shared, ensuring that her spirit lived on in the hearts of those she loved.

Joan's journey through life—a testament to resilience in the face of challenges and a celebration of love and community—serves as a reminder of the enduring bonds that connect us all. Her story is not just one of personal triumphs and trials but also a reflection of the rich tapestry of her heritage, marking her place within the larger narrative of her family and the Jewish community in Kingston.

Raymond Harold "Ray" Kizell[4]

Raymond Harold "Ray" Kizell was born on January 26, 1924. His early years were shaped by the post-World War I era, a time marked by economic challenges and social changes. Growing up as a Jew in Canada, Ray would have been part of a vibrant Jewish community that fostered a strong sense of identity and belonging. The 1920s also saw the emergence of new cultural trends and a sense of optimism, despite the lingering impacts of the war.

RAYMOND HAROLD "RAY" Kizell was just one year old when his sister, Greta, was born on July 11, 1925, in Ontario. As a toddler, Ray would have had limited understanding of the significance of this new addition to the family, but the arrival of a sibling often creates an atmosphere of excitement and joy. Growing up alongside Greta, Ray likely developed a close bond with her, navigating the ups and downs of childhood together.

As they both grew older, their sibling relationship would have been shaped by shared experiences, family gatherings, and the cultural backdrop of their Jewish heritage. The late 1920s and early 1930s were a time of significant change, with the world transitioning into the Great Depression, which had profound effects on families everywhere.

In the Kizell household, the values of resilience and community would have been instilled in Ray and Greta. They learned to appreciate the importance of family, faith, and supporting one another during challenging times. This bond would serve as a foundation for Ray as he navigated his own life's challenges, including the turmoil of World War II and the subsequent quest for stability in a changing world.

Throughout their childhood, Ray and Greta would have enjoyed the simple pleasures of life, such as playing games, sharing stories, and celebrating Jewish traditions together. These formative years would create cherished memories that would last a lifetime, fostering a sense of loyalty and affection that would carry into their adult lives.

As Ray grew, he would have witnessed Greta stepping into her own identity and life path, while he prepared for the significant milestones that awaited him. Their connection as siblings would continue to influence his values and priorities, shaping him into the man he would become in the years to follow.

RAYMOND HAROLD "RAY" Kizell was just three years old when sliced bread was first cut by machine in 1928. This innovation, often regarded as one of the greatest advancements in baking, revolutionized how families consumed bread. For the Kizell family, the availability of pre-sliced bread meant convenience in their daily meals, making it easier to prepare sandwiches and snacks.

Growing up in a Jewish household, Ray would have enjoyed the fresh loaves, likely participating in family meals where bread played a central role in their traditions and customs. This era also saw the introduction of other conveniences that would shape his early memories, such as the rise of consumer products and an increase in access to various foods.

As Ray's world expanded beyond the walls of his home, he would have witnessed the excitement of the Roaring Twenties and the subsequent onset of the Great Depression, which began to affect families across North America in the late 1920s. This juxtaposition of progress and hardship would be a defining backdrop of his early childhood.

By the time he reached school age, the impact of these societal changes would become evident in his education and social interactions. Ray would learn not only academic subjects but also the importance of community and resilience from both his family and his peers during such tumultuous times. The evolution of bread from a staple to a packaged convenience would mirror the transformations in Ray's own life as he adapted to the changing world around him.

These formative experiences would help shape Ray's character and values as he grew older, emphasizing the significance of family, tradition, and adaptability in a rapidly changing society.

IN 1931, WHEN RAYMOND Harold "Ray" Kizell was living in Ottawa, Ontario, the world around him was undergoing significant changes. At just seven years old, he was experiencing life in the Canadian capital during a time of both cultural development and economic challenges.

The Great Depression was beginning to impact Canada, affecting families and communities across the country. Unemployment rates soared, and many families faced financial struggles. In Ottawa, the government was working to address these issues, implementing relief programs to support those in need. Ray's family, like many others, may have felt the effects of these economic hardships, but they likely found comfort in their close-knit community and Jewish traditions.

Despite the difficulties of the time, Ottawa was vibrant with its unique charm. The city was home to many cultural institutions and events that enriched the lives of its residents. Ray would have had access to parks, museums, and local gatherings that reflected the spirit of the community. The Rideau Canal, which ran through the heart of Ottawa, provided a picturesque backdrop for childhood adventures, especially in the winter when it transformed into the world's largest skating rink.

Education was also an important aspect of Ray's life during this period. Attending school in Ottawa, he would have been exposed to a curriculum that emphasized Canadian history, geography, and literature. This educational foundation would play a crucial role in shaping his worldview and understanding of his heritage.

As a young Jewish boy, Ray's upbringing would have included celebrations of Jewish holidays and customs, instilling a sense of identity and community. Family gatherings around the dinner table, sharing traditional meals, would have created cherished memories and a strong connection to his cultural roots.

Living in Ottawa during these formative years, Ray Kizell navigated the complexities of childhood amid economic uncertainty while building the values and connections that would influence him throughout his life.

WHEN RAYMOND HAROLD "Ray" Kizell turned 32 years old in 1956, the world was captivated by the dawn of the space age. The launch of Sputnik by the Soviet Union on October 4, 1957, marked a pivotal moment in history, igniting global interest in space exploration and technological advancement. Although this event occurred a year after his 32nd birthday, the excitement surrounding the impending launch and the advancements in science and technology were already palpable in the air.

Living in Canada, Ray was part of a society that was increasingly focused on modernity and progress. The post-war era saw significant changes as economies rebuilt, and nations sought to innovate. In Canada, the emphasis on education and research was growing, and

Ray may have felt inspired by the developments in engineering and technology that were taking place.

In his personal life, Ray likely experienced both the optimism and challenges of the time. The 1950s were characterized by a sense of consumerism and cultural change, with the rise of television and new forms of entertainment influencing everyday life. Families began to embrace modern conveniences, from appliances to automobiles, and Ray may have enjoyed the benefits of these advancements in his home.

As a Jewish man, he also witnessed a shift in societal attitudes towards diversity and inclusion. The experiences of Jews in Canada were evolving, with a greater emphasis on civil rights and social justice. This period may have prompted Ray to reflect on his heritage and the importance of community, as well as the role of Jewish individuals in shaping the cultural fabric of Canada.

Ray's journey through the early years of the space race would have inspired curiosity about the universe and the possibilities that lay beyond Earth. The launch of Sputnik symbolized not just a technological achievement but also the beginning of a new era where human ambition sought to reach for the stars. Ray, standing at the intersection of history and personal growth, would continue to embrace the changes and challenges that life presented, navigating a world that was rapidly advancing toward the future.

AT 45 YEARS OLD, RAYMOND Harold "Ray" Kizell faced a significant emotional turning point in his life with the passing of his father, Archibald, on August 5, 1969, in Kingston, Ontario. This year was marked by profound changes both in Ray's personal life and the world around him.

The late 1960s were a time of social upheaval and transformation. The world was witnessing the civil rights movement, anti-war protests, and a surge in counterculture as people began to challenge societal norms and advocate for equality and peace. The spirit of rebellion and the desire for change resonated deeply across various communities, including the Jewish community, where discussions around identity, heritage, and social justice were increasingly prominent.

Ray, dealing with the loss of his father, likely found himself reflecting on family legacies and the importance of heritage during this period. Archibald's passing would have prompted him to consider his own role within the family and community. As a Jewish man, he might have drawn strength from his heritage and faith, seeking to honor his father's memory while navigating the evolving social landscape.

The summer of 1969 also saw remarkable events like the Apollo 11 moon landing, where humanity took a giant leap forward, achieving what once seemed impossible. The juxtaposition of personal loss and global triumph might have stirred complex emotions in Ray, as he grappled with the fragility of life while witnessing extraordinary human achievement.

In the wake of Archibald's death, Ray likely turned to family and friends for support, cherishing the bonds that held them together. His experiences during this tumultuous year would shape his perspective on life, legacy, and the importance of community. As he navigated grief, he would also find solace in the memories of his father and the values instilled in him, carrying forward the lessons learned and the love shared within the family.

Ray's journey through this significant chapter would ultimately influence his future endeavors and relationships, fostering a deeper appreciation for the people and experiences that enriched his life as he moved forward in an ever-changing world.

AT 62 YEARS OLD, RAYMOND Harold "Ray" Kizell faced another profound loss with the passing of his brother, Aaron, in Kingston in 1987. This loss would have deeply affected Ray, adding to the grief he had already experienced with the death of their father, Archibald, nearly two decades earlier.

The late 1980s were a time of considerable change in the world, marked by the end of the Cold War and significant advancements in technology and culture. The emotional weight of losing Aaron would have resonated with Ray against this backdrop of shifting global dynamics. As the Jewish community in Canada continued to navigate its identity amidst broader societal changes, Ray might have found solace and support in the traditions and values that had been passed down through their family.

Ray and Aaron likely shared many memories, reflecting the bonds that siblings create throughout their lives. Whether they reminisced about childhood adventures, supported each other through life's challenges, or celebrated family milestones together, the loss of Aaron would have left a significant void in Ray's life.

This period also saw the rise of various social movements, including those advocating for Jewish rights and recognition in Canada. As Ray processed his grief, he might have become more reflective about his own identity and place within the community. The memories of his brother would likely serve as a poignant reminder of the importance of family ties and the need to cherish the moments spent together.

Ray's experiences during this time may have inspired him to strengthen connections with his loved ones, ensuring that the legacy of Aaron—and their shared heritage—continued to resonate within their family. As he navigated the complex emotions tied to loss, Ray might have sought to honor Aaron's memory through acts of kindness, family gatherings, and involvement in the community.

In the face of personal sorrow, the love of family, the warmth of shared traditions, and the lessons learned from their Jewish heritage would serve as guiding lights for Ray as he moved forward, holding onto the cherished memories of his brother while embracing the ever-changing world around him.

AT THE AGE OF 70, RAYMOND Harold "Ray" Kizell witnessed a significant moment in Canadian history when Quebec's sovereignty referendum took place on October 30, 1995. The referendum was a crucial event, as it marked the province's bid for independence from Canada. The rejection of independence by a narrow margin, with 50.58% voting against it, stirred various emotions across the nation and sparked conversations about national identity, regionalism, and cultural heritage.

For Ray, who had lived through various transformative periods in both Canadian and Jewish history, this political moment may have brought reflections on the themes of unity and belonging. Growing up in Ontario and identifying as part of the Jewish community, he might have felt a deep connection to the ongoing discussions about what it meant to be Canadian, especially as a member of a minority group.

As the son of Jewish immigrants, Ray likely appreciated the diversity that Canada represented, while also recognizing the complexities that came with it. The political climate of the 1990s, with its debates around language rights, multiculturalism, and provincial autonomy, may have resonated with his own experiences of navigating identity and heritage. Ray might have felt a sense of pride in Canada's commitment to a multicultural society, even as he reflected on the challenges faced by different communities, including his own.

In this year, Ray could have engaged in discussions with family and friends about the implications of the referendum results, contemplating what a different Quebec could have meant for their lives and the Jewish community at large. He may have also taken the opportunity to participate in local community events, fostering connections among diverse groups and advocating for understanding and cooperation among different cultures.

As Ray approached the later years of his life, he likely valued the importance of passing on stories of resilience and heritage to the next generations. The discussions surrounding Quebec's independence may have inspired him to share insights from his own family's journey, emphasizing the significance of staying connected to their roots while embracing the evolving landscape of Canada.

With the backdrop of such a pivotal moment in Canadian history, Ray might have felt motivated to reflect on his legacy, ensuring that the values of community, togetherness, and cultural pride would continue to thrive within his family, regardless of the political winds that shaped their nation.

AT THE AGE OF 71, RAYMOND Harold "Ray" Kizell faced the emotional loss of his sister Doris, who passed away on January 4, 1996, in Kingston. Doris, who had been a significant presence in Ray's life, was not only his sibling but also a companion who shared the journey of growing up in a Jewish household in Ontario.

Her passing marked a poignant moment for Ray, bringing with it a flood of memories from their childhood in Ottawa and the bond they had developed over the years. Growing up together during a time of significant historical events, including the Great Depression and the Second World War, their shared experiences fostered a deep connection. Doris had always been a source of support for Ray, and losing her meant the end of an era in their family.

As he navigated through his grief, Ray likely found comfort in recalling fond memories of Doris: family gatherings, holidays, and the laughter they shared during their youth. He may have taken time to reflect on the values they were raised with—family, resilience, and faith—strengthening his resolve to honor her memory.

In the days following her death, Ray may have participated in rituals and traditions associated with mourning in the Jewish faith, seeking solace in community support. The Kaddish, a prayer for the deceased, would have offered him a way to connect spiritually with Doris and keep her memory alive. Surrounded by family and friends, he would have shared stories that celebrated Doris's life, perhaps bringing to light her achievements and the joy she brought to those around her.

In the context of the ongoing discussions about identity and community, Doris's death may have prompted Ray to consider the importance of familial connections in maintaining cultural heritage. He might have felt an urgency to pass down their family's stories, ensuring that the next generation understood the sacrifices made and the love shared among them.

As he mourned his sister, Ray also reflected on the broader tapestry of his family's history, finding strength in the knowledge that their legacy continued through him and his loved ones. The experience of loss, while painful, could have deepened his appreciation for life, prompting him to cherish the time spent with his remaining family members, particularly as they gathered to remember Doris and celebrate her impact on their lives.

AT THE AGE OF 79, RAYMOND Harold "Ray" Kizell passed away in Kingston on May 31, 2003. His passing marked the end of a remarkable life filled with rich experiences, familial connections, and a deep sense of community.

Ray lived through significant historical events, from the Great Depression to the rise of technology in the late 20th century, shaping his worldview and personal beliefs. He navigated the challenges and triumphs of his era, embracing his Jewish heritage while also adapting to the changing times around him.

In the years leading up to his death, Ray had likely become a cherished figure in his family, offering wisdom and guidance to younger generations. He was known for sharing stories of his childhood, his experiences during World War II, and the values instilled in him by his parents, Archibald and a strong family legacy that included his siblings, Doris and Aaron.

Ray's life was characterized by his commitment to family and community. He and his wife, Joan, shared a loving partnership, supporting each other through the ups and downs of life. As they navigated the joys and sorrows of aging together, they created a warm home filled with laughter and memories. Ray's loss would have left a profound impact on those who knew him, especially Joan, who had stood by his side through many of life's challenges.

After Ray's passing, his family gathered to honor his memory and celebrate the life he lived. They reflected on his love for them and the values he imparted. Sharing stories and reminiscing about cherished moments spent together became a way for them to keep his spirit alive.

As they honored his legacy, Ray's family also recognized the importance of passing down the traditions and history of their Jewish heritage. They likely took comfort in the knowledge that, although he was no longer physically present, his lessons, love, and the stories of their family's history would continue to be shared and cherished by future generations.

Ray was laid to rest in Beth Israel Cemetery, a place where family members could visit and remember the man who had so profoundly influenced their lives. In the quiet of the cemetery, as they visited his grave, they could reflect on his contributions to their lives and the legacy he left behind—a testament to the enduring bonds of family, faith, and history.

Louis Langbort[5]

Louis Langport was born in 1882, a year marked by significant social and technological changes across the globe. In the late 19th century, the world was experiencing the effects of the Industrial Revolution, which had begun a few decades earlier. This era saw rapid urbanization as people moved from rural areas to cities in search of work, leading to a population shift and significant changes in lifestyles.

Global Context of 1882:

1. Technological Advancements: The Second Industrial Revolution was in full swing, bringing about innovations in steel production, electrical engineering, and chemical processes. The telephone, invented by Alexander Graham Bell in 1876, was becoming more widespread, facilitating better communication.

2. SOCIAL CHANGES: The era was marked by a rise in social movements advocating for labor rights and reforms. Workers began organizing into unions to fight for better working conditions, wages, and hours. This was particularly important in industrial cities, where labor exploitation was rampant.

3. CULTURAL SHIFTS: The arts were flourishing, with movements such as Impressionism and the rise of Modernism. Writers like Leo Tolstoy and Mark Twain were producing influential works that would shape literature for generations.

4. POLITICAL LANDSCAPE: The year also witnessed significant political events, such as the British annexation of Egypt, reflecting the ongoing imperial expansions of European powers. In the United States, the aftermath of the Civil War was still felt, with the nation grappling with issues of race and reconstruction.

5. JEWISH LIFE: FOR Jewish communities, 1882 was a complex time. Many Jews in Eastern Europe faced discrimination, pogroms, and restrictive laws that limited their rights. In contrast, Jewish immigrants were arriving in the United States, seeking refuge from persecution and the promise of better opportunities. This year saw a surge in Jewish migration, particularly from Russia and Poland, leading to the establishment of vibrant Jewish communities in American cities.

EARLY LIFE FOR LOUIS Langport:

Born into this transformative world, Louis Langport's early life would have been shaped by these prevailing trends. If he were born into a Jewish family, he likely experienced the cultural richness and religious traditions of Jewish life, alongside the challenges faced by his community.

As he grew, he would have witnessed the profound changes of the early 20th century, which would impact not only his personal life but also the broader Jewish experience in North America or wherever he may have settled. The tensions and opportunities of his time would lay the groundwork for the values, challenges, and aspirations that defined his life and the lives of future generations in his family.

LOUIS LANGPORT WAS six years old in 1888, the year that marked a significant advancement in photography with the introduction of the Kodak camera by George Eastman. This invention was revolutionary, making photography accessible to the general public for the first time. Here's what life might have been like for Louis during this transformative period:

Life in 1888:

1. The Kodak Camera:

The Kodak camera came preloaded with film for 100 exposures and included a simple instruction manual that encouraged users to "take the picture and send it back." This democratization of photography allowed families to document their lives, capture memories, and express themselves creatively. For Louis and his family, this innovation may have meant more opportunities to preserve their heritage and everyday life through photographs.

2. SOCIAL AND CULTURAL Context:

The late 19th century was characterized by rapid industrial growth and urbanization. Cities were expanding, and so were the immigrant populations, including Jewish communities fleeing persecution in Eastern Europe. As a Jewish boy, Louis may have experienced a blend of traditional Jewish culture and the new, modern influences coming from the surrounding society.

3. EDUCATION AND CHILDHOOD:

In 1888, education for children was becoming more standardized, with many children attending school regularly. Louis would likely have been receiving a basic education, learning reading, writing, and arithmetic, along with the cultural and religious teachings of his family.

4. FAMILY LIFE:

Family was central to Jewish culture, and traditions played an important role in daily life. Louis may have participated in celebrations and rituals that reinforced his family's identity and values, such as Shabbat dinners, holidays, and other community gatherings.

5. TECHNOLOGICAL INFLUENCE:

Beyond photography, the late 1880s saw significant advancements in other areas as well, such as transportation with the expansion of the railroad network and electric streetcars. These developments made travel easier and helped connect communities, which was especially important for immigrant populations like Louis's family.

6. POLITICAL CLIMATE:

The rise of anti-Semitic sentiments in various parts of Europe might have created an atmosphere of tension for Jewish families. While some were seeking better lives in America, others faced harsh realities, including poverty and discrimination.

Louis's Growing World:

As Louis grew, the availability of photography would likely become a cherished way to document his life and those of his family and friends. This technological breakthrough aligned with his formative years, helping shape his perspective on the world and the importance of capturing and preserving memories.

The combination of cultural heritage, new technologies, and the challenges faced by Jewish communities during this era would have influenced his upbringing and the values he carried into adulthood. As a young Jewish boy in a rapidly changing world, Louis was poised to navigate the complexities of modern life, balancing tradition with innovation as he moved forward in the 20th century.

―――――――

LOUIS LANGPORT WAS 16 years old in 1896 when the first modern Olympic Games were held in Athens, Greece. This monumental event marked a significant revival of the ancient tradition of the Olympics and was filled with excitement and international enthusiasm. Here's what life may have been like for Louis during this pivotal year:

Life in 1896:

1. The Revival of the Olympics:

The 1896 Olympics, organized by Pierre de Coubertin, featured athletes from 13 nations competing in 43 events, including track and field, wrestling, and gymnastics. The event sparked a renewed interest in sports and physical education across the globe. For a young man like Louis, this might have been an inspiring moment, showcasing the spirit of competition and international camaraderie.

2. CULTURAL AND SOCIAL Context:

The late 19th century was a period of great change. The Industrial Revolution had transformed economies and societies, leading to urbanization and changes in lifestyles. Jewish communities were actively engaged in these changes, adapting to new social dynamics while preserving their cultural identity.

3. INTEREST IN SPORTS:

The rise of organized sports was becoming more pronounced. Athletic clubs were being established, and various sports were gaining popularity. Louis may have been inspired to participate in sports or join local athletic clubs, enjoying the camaraderie and physical activity that accompanied this emerging cultural trend.

4. EDUCATION AND OPPORTUNITIES:

As a teenager, Louis would likely have been continuing his education, possibly attending a secondary school or trade school. The growing emphasis on education and literacy in Jewish communities meant that young people were increasingly encouraged to pursue academic and professional opportunities.

5. GLOBAL AWARENESS:

The Olympics were a global event, and the coverage of the games would have reached many, including Louis. The international nature of the Olympics may have sparked his interest in the wider world, encouraging him to think beyond local concerns and consider global events and cultures.

---

6. POLITICAL CLIMATE:

In 1896, anti-Semitic sentiments were still prevalent in various parts of Europe, and many Jewish families were navigating the complexities of identity and belonging. The Olympics could have provided a temporary escape for Louis, a chance to focus on sports and celebration rather than the societal challenges facing his community.

Louis's Perspective:

At 16, Louis was on the cusp of adulthood, eager to explore the world and his place within it. The excitement of the Olympic Games, coupled with the backdrop of a rapidly changing society, would have influenced his aspirations and dreams. Engaging in sports, connecting with friends, and witnessing the celebration of human achievement could have served as important influences as he began to define his identity and future in a world full of possibilities.

As he moved into adulthood, the values of competition, teamwork, and perseverance highlighted by the Olympics might resonate with him, shaping his character and ambitions in the years to come. This period of his life would lay the groundwork for the man he would become, as he navigated the complexities of being a Jewish immigrant in an evolving society while embracing the spirit of progress that defined his youth.

LOUIS LANGPORT WAS 21 years old in 1903 when the Wright brothers made their historic powered flight at Kitty Hawk, North Carolina. This groundbreaking achievement was a pivotal moment in the history of aviation and had significant implications for transportation and technology. Here's what life may have been like for Louis during this exciting year:

Life in 1903:

1. The Wright Brothers' Achievement:

On December 17, 1903, Orville and Wilbur Wright successfully flew the first powered airplane, the Wright Flyer, covering 120 feet in 12 seconds. This monumental event marked the beginning of the aviation age, inspiring a sense of wonder and possibility in people worldwide.

For Louis, witnessing such an extraordinary milestone might have sparked his imagination and aspirations regarding technology and innovation.

---

2. CULTURAL SHIFT:

The early 20th century was a time of rapid advancement and optimism. Innovations in technology were transforming daily life, from the rise of automobiles to the expansion of the telegraph and telephone. Louis would have experienced a sense of excitement as these advancements made the world feel smaller and more interconnected.

---

3. IMPACT ON SOCIETY:

The advent of powered flight would eventually change the landscape of travel and commerce. Although commercial aviation was still decades away, the idea of flying captured the public's imagination and laid the groundwork for future developments in transportation. As a young man, Louis might have considered the implications of flight on trade, travel, and human connection.

---

4. PERSONAL ASPIRATIONS:

At 21, Louis was likely contemplating his future and exploring various opportunities. The success of the Wright brothers may have inspired him to think about his aspirations, whether in engineering, business, or other fields influenced by technological advancements. It was a time to dream about what the future could hold.

---

5. SOCIAL CHANGES:

The early 1900s also saw significant social changes, including the suffrage movement gaining momentum and labor rights being discussed more openly. Jewish communities, like others, were increasingly engaging in social issues, advocating for equality and justice. This societal backdrop may have encouraged Louis to think critically about his place in the community and the broader world.

6. THE JEWISH EXPERIENCE:

For Louis, as a young Jewish man, these years were crucial for exploring his identity amidst changing social dynamics. While facing the challenges of anti-Semitism, many in the Jewish community were finding ways to contribute to society and assert their identities. The excitement surrounding technological advancements might have provided a sense of hope and a desire for progress.

Louis's Perspective:

As a 21-year-old, Louis Langport was poised on the brink of adulthood, filled with the hopes and dreams characteristic of youth. The achievement of the Wright brothers could have inspired him to envision a future where innovation and possibility were within reach. Engaging with the advancements of the time, he might have felt empowered to pursue his passions, whether they lay in technology, entrepreneurship, or social advocacy.

The historic flight served as a reminder that human ingenuity knows no bounds and that the pursuit of dreams is often fraught with challenges but ultimately rewarding. This year marked a significant moment not only in aviation history but also in Louis's own journey toward adulthood, as he began to carve out his identity in a world increasingly shaped by innovation and the relentless pursuit of progress.

———————————

LOUIS LANGPORT WAS 50 years old in 1932, a year when Joseph Stalin's regime intensified its grip on the Soviet Union, resulting in widespread terror and famine. While Louis was living in Canada, the global political climate was deeply affected by these events, and here's how this tumultuous period might have influenced him and his surroundings:

Life in 1932:

1. Stalin's Policies:

In 1932, Stalin's policies, particularly the forced collectivization of agriculture, led to devastating famine in Ukraine and other regions. Millions suffered from starvation, and the regime's oppressive tactics aimed at consolidating power resulted in the arrest, execution, or exile of countless individuals. While Louis may not have been directly affected, the news of these horrors would have reached Canadian shores, raising concerns within the Jewish community and beyond about the state of human rights and freedoms.

---

2. IMPACT ON JEWISH Communities:

The rise of totalitarian regimes in Europe, including Stalin's USSR, instilled fear among Jewish populations, especially in Eastern Europe. Many Jewish families were deeply concerned about the implications of Stalin's policies and the potential for persecution. This growing anxiety could have prompted Louis and his peers to reflect on their own community's safety and the importance of standing against tyranny.

---

3. GROWING AWARENESS of Global Events:

In the early 1930s, the world was grappling with the economic fallout of the Great Depression, which began in 1929. Many Canadians were feeling the effects of unemployment and economic instability. News of international events, including Stalin's terror, likely heightened the sense of urgency to support those facing hardship. Louis may have been motivated to engage in community efforts to assist those in need, recognizing the interconnectedness of human struggles.

---

4. CULTURAL SHIFT:

The 1930s were also marked by artistic and cultural movements that sought to address social issues and promote change. As a member of the Jewish community, Louis may have found inspiration in literature, music, and the arts that highlighted the fight against oppression and celebrated cultural identity. This period fostered a sense of solidarity and resilience among marginalized groups, including Jews.

---

5. PERSONAL REFLECTION:

At 50, Louis may have been reflecting on his own life choices and the legacy he wished to leave. The political climate could have sparked a deeper interest in advocacy, prompting him to consider how he could contribute to his community and support efforts for social justice. His experiences as a Jewish man in Canada might have driven him to engage in dialogue about the importance of tolerance and understanding in an increasingly divided world.

---

6. RESPONSES TO CRISIS:

Many Jewish organizations in Canada were mobilizing to provide aid to those affected by the famine and terror in the Soviet Union. Louis may have participated in fundraising efforts or community discussions aimed at raising awareness about the plight of those suffering under Stalin's regime. This sense of communal responsibility could have strengthened his ties to fellow Jews and reinforced the importance of collective action.

Louis's Perspective:

As Louis Langport navigated his 50th year, the impact of global events like Stalin's terror and the economic struggles of the Great Depression likely weighed heavily on his mind. He may have felt a sense of urgency to address the injustices he saw around him, both locally and internationally

LOUIS LANGPORT PASSED away in Kingston, Ontario, in 1933 at the age of 51, leaving behind a legacy shaped by the tumultuous events of his time and his experiences as a member of the Jewish community. His burial in Beth Israel Cemetery signifies not only a physical resting place but also a connection to a rich heritage and the enduring memories of those who came before him.

Life After Louis Langport's Passing:

1. Historical Context:

Louis's death in 1933 occurred during a period of significant change, not only in Canada but globally. This year was marked by the rise of totalitarian regimes in Europe, including the consolidation of power by Adolf Hitler in Germany. The world was becoming increasingly aware of the threats posed to minority communities, particularly Jews, in many parts of Europe.

2. COMMUNITY RESPONSE:

After Louis's passing, the Jewish community in Kingston would have come together to mourn his loss, honoring his contributions and remembering his life. The burial at Beth Israel Cemetery provided a space for communal grief and reflection, as family and friends gathered to pay their respects and celebrate his legacy.

---

3. LEGACY OF RESILIENCE:

Louis's life, marked by both personal achievements and the challenges of his era, would serve as an example of resilience for future generations. His experiences as a Jewish immigrant in Canada, navigating a world filled with adversity, could inspire others to appreciate the importance of cultural identity and community support.

---

4. FAMILY AND CONTINUITY:

Louis's passing would have a profound impact on his family. His children and relatives, while grappling with their loss, would carry forward the values he instilled in them—values of perseverance, compassion, and commitment to social justice. The lessons learned from Louis's life could echo through their actions and decisions, contributing to the ongoing story of their family.

---

5. CULTURAL MEMORY:

Over time, the memory of Louis Langport would likely be preserved through family stories, photographs, and records. His descendants might share tales of his life, his struggles, and his contributions to the community, ensuring that his spirit remains alive within the family narrative. These recollections would serve as a reminder of the importance of remembering one's roots and honoring those who came before.

6. BETH ISRAEL CEMETERY:

The choice of burial in Beth Israel Cemetery reflects the strong ties to Jewish identity and community. This sacred ground serves not only as a resting place for the deceased but also as a symbol of the resilience of the Jewish people in Canada. As more individuals were laid to rest there, the cemetery would grow to represent the rich tapestry of Jewish life in Kingston, a testament to the community's history and continuity.

Final Reflection:

Louis Langport's life and passing serve as poignant reminders of the complexities of identity, belonging, and resilience. His story, intertwined with the broader narrative of Jewish history in Canada, reflects the enduring struggle for acceptance and the celebration of cultural heritage. As the years go by, the impact of his life will continue to resonate through the lives of those he touched and the legacy he left behind—a legacy rooted in hope, community, and a commitment to justice. His resting place at Beth Israel Cemetery will stand as a tribute to the journey he undertook and the lessons learned along the way, inviting future generations to reflect on their heritage and the importance of standing firm in the face of adversity.

Annie Longbort[6]

Annie Langport's passing in Kingston, Ontario, on May 28, 1942, marked the end of a life that had been lived through a period of profound historical shifts and challenges. As a Jewish woman, Annie would have seen a world where change was constant—navigating societal transformations and enduring the early 20th-century's most defining moments. Her burial in Beth Israel Cemetery links her life to a place that stands as a testament to the lives and legacies of Kingston's Jewish community.

Life at the Time of Annie's Passing

1. A World at War:

Annie passed away during World War II, a time when global conflict reached unprecedented levels, affecting people across nations and cultures. Although Canada was far from the battles, Canadian forces and citizens were heavily engaged in the war effort, and news of the horrors unfolding in Europe deeply affected Jewish communities worldwide. The global Jewish diaspora, including communities in Canada, were heartbroken by news of the plight of Jewish families in Europe, facing widespread persecution. Annie's death in 1942 meant she would not witness the liberation that came with the end of the war, but her life was a piece of the strength that kept her community together.

2. THE JEWISH COMMUNITY in Kingston:

The Jewish community in Kingston in the early 1940s would have been relatively small but tightly knit. Like many Jewish communities in Canada, it was formed by families who had emigrated to North America for better opportunities or to escape persecution in Europe. By the time Annie passed, Beth Israel Congregation had become a center for Jewish life in Kingston, where families gathered for religious services, festivals, and social events, fostering a sense of identity and support amidst the backdrop of a world at war.

3. Canadian Society in the 1940s:

In 1942, Canada was heavily involved in the war effort, and the country was mobilized on many fronts—industries retooled to support the production of war supplies, and communities organized events to raise funds and morale. Many Canadian men, including Jewish Canadians, were serving overseas, and the country was united in the war effort. This era was also marked by food rationing, blackouts, and a heightened sense of national duty. For Jewish Canadians, it was a time of complex emotions: solidarity with fellow citizens but deep concern for Jewish relatives abroad.

4. ANNIE'S LEGACY AND Resting Place:

With her burial in Beth Israel Cemetery, Annie Langport became part of Kingston's enduring Jewish heritage. Her gravestone would join those of other members of the community, forming a tapestry of individual stories that together tell the history of Jewish life in Kingston. Her legacy reflects not only her personal journey but also the experiences of Jewish immigrants in Canada, who helped shape communities while holding fast to their cultural and religious identities.

Beth Israel Cemetery, where Annie was laid to rest, continues to be a meaningful place for families and descendants, preserving the memories of the individuals who contributed to Kingston's Jewish legacy. Annie's life and burial there remind us of the resilience and strength of those who lived through turbulent times, providing a historical anchor for future generations seeking to understand their roots.

Esther Longbort[7]

Esther Longbort's passing on March 7, 1943, in Kingston, Ontario, came amid one of the most intense periods of World War II. Just like her relative, Annie, Esther's life would have been shaped by the backdrop of world events, her faith, and the close-knit community in Kingston. Her burial in Beth Israel Cemetery added another chapter to the fabric of the local Jewish heritage, with each grave marker preserving the memory of those who lived through times of great change.

In 1943, the Jewish community in Canada was deeply affected by the war. News of atrocities against Jews in Europe had begun to circulate, stirring profound concern and sadness. Canadian Jewish communities were actively involved in raising funds and supporting the war effort, hoping to contribute to a future where peace and security would prevail for everyone, especially for those of Jewish heritage abroad. Esther's community would have been particularly focused on supporting both Jewish soldiers in the Canadian Armed Forces and refugees escaping war-torn Europe, despite the restrictive immigration policies Canada upheld at that time.

Beth Israel Cemetery, where Esther was laid to rest, had become a place not only of remembrance but of resilience. Each individual laid to rest there, including Esther, represents the perseverance of Jewish families who settled in Canada, contributing to a broader narrative of endurance and cultural pride. Today, Esther's grave serves as a testament to her life, connecting future generations to the past and reminding them of the contributions and sacrifices made by their ancestors.

Dr. Samuel Ludwin[8]

———

Dr. Samuel Ludwin's birth on October 16, 1944, in Johannesburg, South Africa, took place during a pivotal year in world history, as World War II neared its end. South Africa, part of the British Commonwealth, was actively involved in the war, contributing troops, supplies, and medical expertise to support the Allies.

For South Africa's Jewish community, 1944 was a time of concern for loved ones in Europe and a period of active support for the war effort. Many Jewish South Africans, especially those with Eastern European roots, had relatives abroad, and the community organized relief efforts and support networks in response to the global crisis. Despite these challenges, Johannesburg's Jewish population continued to thrive, maintaining their synagogues, schools, and community centers.

South African society, already divided along racial lines, had yet to formally enter the apartheid era, which would begin in 1948. However, Jewish South Africans lived within a society where race and identity held defining roles. Jewish communities, often tightly knit, emphasized values of education, professional success, and cultural preservation.

Dr. Ludwin's early years unfolded in a vibrant, resilient Jewish community within a complex social and political environment—one that would shape his values before he eventually went on to make his mark in the medical and academic fields.

———

AT AGE 10, DR. SAMUEL Ludwin witnessed South Africa's withdrawal from UNESCO in 1954. This was a significant moment in the country's history, reflecting the beginning of its increasing isolation from international organizations due to the policies of racial segregation under apartheid.

South Africa's decision to quit UNESCO came as a response to international condemnation of its apartheid policies, which discriminated against non-white South Africans in nearly every aspect of life. UNESCO's commitment to human rights and equality was in direct conflict with the South African government's stance, leading to a growing divide between South Africa and the international community. For the country's Jewish population, this era marked a period of reflection and concern. Many within the community opposed apartheid and were outspoken about human rights issues, contributing to the emerging voices of opposition against the government's oppressive policies.

Growing up during this period, Samuel would have been aware of the tension and complexities within his society.

AT 31, DR. SAMUEL LUDWIN lived through a pivotal and tragic event in South African history—the Soweto Uprising on June 16, 1976. This day marked a turning point in the anti-apartheid struggle, igniting widespread protest and global condemnation of South Africa's policies. The uprising began as a student protest against the government's mandate that Afrikaans, the language associated with apartheid and oppression, be used in schools. When police opened fire on the young protestors, the violent response and tragic loss of life quickly escalated the incident, drawing international attention and sparking demonstrations and strikes across the country.

As a South African Jew, Samuel would have likely been deeply affected by this period. Many members of the Jewish community opposed apartheid and were involved in social justice causes. This tragedy underscored the urgent need for change, as the brutal response illustrated the depth of government oppression. For Samuel, who would eventually build a career in academia and medicine, these formative years in South Africa may have shaped his outlook on equity, human rights, and community, driving a commitment to making a difference wherever he could.

WHEN DR. SAMUEL LUDWIN was 49 years old, Nelson Mandela was inaugurated as President of South Africa on May 10, 1994, marking a historic moment in both South African and global history. This event symbolized the end of apartheid and the beginning of a new era of democracy, equality, and hope for the nation. For those who had witnessed apartheid's harshest years, including those who had left South Africa, Mandela's presidency felt like the realization of a dream many thought they might never see.

As a South African expatriate, Samuel would likely have felt both pride and a sense of healing for his homeland as Mandela took office. The joy and relief extended far beyond South Africa's borders, resonating with the international community and embodying a triumph of resilience and justice. Mandela's leadership promised a rebirth for the country, and for Samuel, this moment may have been an inspiring reminder of the power of perseverance, justice, and the importance of nurturing one's roots, no matter where life may lead.

AT THE AGE OF 75, DR. Samuel Ludwin passed away on January 21, 2020, in Kingston, Ontario. His final resting place is in Beth Israel Cemetery, surrounded by the community and legacy he contributed to throughout his life. Dr. Ludwin, a Jewish South African by birth who later made Canada his home, leaves behind a narrative of resilience, cross-cultural roots, and a lifelong dedication to medicine and education. His life spanned significant historical moments, from apartheid to South Africa's transformation, and his work touched countless lives, leaving a lasting impact on those who knew him and on the communities he served.

Dr. Ludwin's story stands as a bridge between the challenges of his birthplace and the diverse opportunities he embraced in Canada, where his legacy is honored among family, friends, and colleagues who remember him with respect and affection.

Ella Marcus[9]

Ella Marcus was born on June 5, 1919, in Quebec, a time when Canada, like much of the world, was experiencing a period of transition and challenge. The year 1919 marked the end of World War I, bringing both relief and the deep impacts of wartime loss, which affected communities nationwide. Many families mourned lost loved ones, while others celebrated the homecoming of soldiers. The government was addressing new challenges, including veterans' reintegration and rising labor disputes, as returning soldiers struggled to find work in a post-war economy.

For Quebec's Jewish community, 1919 was a time of growth and community-building. Jewish immigrants continued arriving from Europe, bringing their culture and traditions while also facing the reality of antisemitism and adjusting to life in Canada. Montreal, in particular, became a cultural hub for Jewish Canadians, with institutions like synagogues and community organizations growing in influence. Although women's roles were largely limited, the suffragist movement was gaining momentum, with women in Canada (excluding Quebec) recently granted the right to vote federally in 1918. This political shift inspired hope and would eventually lead to greater rights for women across the country, including Quebec.

ELLA MARCUS WAS 6 YEARS old when her brother, Samuel David, was born on September 18, 1925. Growing up in a family that valued creativity and cultural heritage, Ella likely took on a nurturing role with her younger brother. Their shared childhood experiences in Quebec during the 1920s would have been filled with the vibrancy of family gatherings, community celebrations, and the exploration of their Jewish identity.

As Samuel grew, Ella's influence as an older sister may have sparked his own interests, perhaps in the arts or other creative endeavors. The siblings would have shared the challenges and joys of their upbringing, navigating the complexities of life during the interwar years—a time marked by significant social and political changes. The bond they formed during those formative years likely played a crucial role in shaping their individual paths.

Ella's artistic journey and Samuel's life would have intersected as they supported one another through their respective endeavors. Samuel, inspired by his sister's passion for art, might have pursued his own interests, contributing to the family's artistic legacy. Their relationship reflects the importance of sibling connections, especially in a time when families often relied on one another for support and encouragement in their pursuits.

ELLA MARCUS WAS 22 years old when her mother, Leah, passed away in Kingston, Ontario, on July 28, 1941. The loss of Leah, a guiding figure in Ella's life, would have been a profound moment for her. Having grown up in a Jewish household, the values and traditions instilled by her mother likely shaped Ella's identity and artistic vision.

Leah's passing during a tumultuous time in history—World War II was unfolding—may have added to the emotional weight of the loss. The world was filled with uncertainty, and as Ella navigated her early adulthood, she would have faced not only her grief but also the larger societal changes impacting her community and family.

Ella's relationship with her mother, characterized by love and shared experiences, would have provided her with a foundation to draw upon as she continued to develop her artistic talents. This pivotal moment could have fueled a deeper connection to her creative work, perhaps inspiring her to honor Leah's memory through her art. The pain of losing her mother might have also driven Ella to seek solace and meaning in her creative endeavors, reflecting her experiences and emotions on canvas.

As she moved forward in life, the absence of her mother would likely have influenced her relationships and her approach to family, possibly inspiring her to create a nurturing environment for others, much like Leah had done for her. Ella's journey as an artist would be intertwined with the memory of her mother, shaping her perspective and commitment to preserving their cultural heritage through her art.

ELLA MARCUS WAS 29 years old when Canada became a founding member of NATO in 1949. This year marked a significant shift in global politics, as the North Atlantic Treaty Organization was established to provide collective security against the threat of Soviet aggression during the Cold War.

For Ella, living in Kingston, Ontario, the implications of NATO's formation would have resonated deeply, especially given the ongoing recovery from World War II and the emerging tensions of the post-war era. As an artist, she may have found inspiration in the themes of unity and cooperation that NATO represented. The formation of this alliance could have sparked discussions in her community about national identity, security, and the importance of solidarity among democratic nations.

Ella, navigating her late twenties, was at a crucial point in her life, likely exploring her artistic voice while contemplating her role in a rapidly changing world. The geopolitical landscape influenced by NATO could have inspired her art, as she sought to reflect the hopes and anxieties of her generation in her creative works.

Moreover, being part of a society that was increasingly aware of its international responsibilities may have encouraged Ella to engage with broader themes in her artwork, such as peace, freedom, and the interconnectedness of cultures. The year 1949 would mark not only a pivotal moment in global history but also a formative period in Ella's development as an artist, as she continued to find her voice amid the changing tides of her time.

───────

ELLA MARCUS WAS 40 years old when Canada's first Bill of Rights was introduced in 1960. This legislation marked a significant milestone in the country's legal and cultural history, as it established protections for fundamental freedoms and rights, including freedom of speech, religion, and assembly.

For Ella, living in Kingston, Ontario, this was an empowering moment that resonated deeply with her artistic sensibilities. As an artist, she would have been acutely aware of the importance of civil liberties, especially during a time when many societal movements were advocating for equality and justice. The introduction of the Bill of Rights may have inspired her to explore themes of freedom and human rights in her artwork, reflecting the spirit of progress and change that characterized the era.

In the 1960s, Canada was undergoing significant social transformation, with voices rising for greater equality across various demographics, including women, Indigenous peoples, and racial minorities. Ella, as a Jewish woman, might have felt a personal connection to these struggles, leading her to use her art as a platform for expression and advocacy.

Her work during this period may have been influenced by the broader cultural shifts, as artists sought to engage with social issues and provoke thought through their creations. The introduction of the Bill of Rights could have served as a catalyst for Ella to participate in the conversations surrounding social justice, perhaps collaborating with other artists or engaging with community initiatives that aimed to promote awareness and change.

As she embraced this new era of rights and freedoms, Ella's art likely reflected a commitment to exploring the complexities of identity, belonging, and the ongoing fight for justice. This period would be pivotal not only for her personal development but also for the broader movement toward equality and human rights in Canada.

ELLA MARCUS WAS 42 years old when Saskatchewan Medicare set a prototype for all provinces in Canada in 1962. This landmark development was a pivotal moment in Canadian history, as it established a publicly funded healthcare system that would later inspire the nationwide implementation of universal healthcare.

Living in Kingston, Ontario, Ella would have witnessed firsthand the discussions and debates surrounding this significant reform. The introduction of Medicare in Saskatchewan symbolized a commitment to social welfare and the belief that healthcare is a fundamental right for all citizens, regardless of their economic status.

As an artist during this transformative period, Ella might have been inspired by the values embodied in the Medicare movement. The push for accessible healthcare aligned with her experiences and the growing awareness of social justice issues, reinforcing the importance of community support and compassion in society. Her artwork may have reflected themes of health and wellness, portraying the human experience and the need for equitable access to medical care.

Ella's involvement in the art community could have led her to collaborate with healthcare advocates, using her platform to raise awareness about the importance of Medicare and the necessity of healthcare reform across Canada. Her pieces might have conveyed the struggles of individuals navigating the healthcare system, emphasizing the disparities and challenges faced by marginalized communities.

As the Medicare model gained traction and eventually became a core value of Canadian identity, Ella would have likely celebrated this progress in her art, capturing the spirit of hope and resilience that accompanied such significant change. This period marked not only a milestone in healthcare but also a reflection of Ella's evolving role as an artist dedicated to advocating for social justice through her creative expression.

Ella's experiences and the impact of Saskatchewan Medicare would continue to influence her artistic journey as she navigated the complexities of a society increasingly focused on equality, human rights, and the fundamental dignity of all individuals.

IN 1974, ELLA MARCUS had established herself as an artist, immersing herself in the vibrant artistic community of Quebec. This was a dynamic time for artists in Canada, as the country was experiencing a cultural renaissance, fueled by an increasing interest in indigenous and multicultural perspectives in art. The 1970s saw a surge in artistic expression across various mediums, including painting, sculpture, and mixed media.

As a Jewish woman and an artist, Ella contributed to this movement, drawing inspiration from her heritage and the rich tapestry of life around her. Her work often reflected themes of identity, resilience, and the intersection of personal and cultural history, resonating with many who experienced similar journeys.

During this period, the Quebec government was also promoting arts and culture through initiatives like the Ministère des Affaires culturelles, which sought to support and nurture local talent. Ella likely participated in exhibitions, showcasing her work in galleries and community spaces, and perhaps engaging with fellow artists in collective projects.

Her artistic endeavors not only allowed her to express herself but also to connect with others in the community, creating a network of support and collaboration that defined the artistic landscape of Quebec during the 1970s. This was a transformative decade for Ella, as she navigated both her personal and professional identities, making a lasting impact on the local art scene.

———

ELLA WAS 55 YEARS OLD when her brother, Samuel David, passed away in Kingston, Ontario, on January 30, 1975. His death would have profoundly affected her, marking a significant loss in her life. The bond between siblings often holds deep emotional significance, and Ella likely felt the weight of that connection acutely in the wake of his passing.

Samuel's death occurred during a period of social and political change in Canada, and Ella may have channeled her grief into her art. As an artist, she could have explored themes of loss, memory, and resilience in her work, creating pieces that reflected her personal experiences and the universal struggle of coping with the death of a loved one. This period might have prompted her to reflect on their childhood memories, shared experiences, and the unique relationship they had cultivated over the years.

In the wake of Samuel's passing, Ella may have sought solace in her art, using it as a means to express her emotions and honor her brother's memory. She might have painted portraits of him or created works that captured the essence of their sibling bond, intertwining her personal narrative with broader themes of love and loss. The grief she experienced could have deepened her understanding of the human experience, allowing her to create art that resonated with others who had faced similar losses.

Ella's connections within the Kingston arts community might have provided her with a support system during this challenging time. Friends and fellow artists may have rallied around her, offering comfort and companionship as she navigated her grief. Her experiences with loss could have also fueled her desire to connect with others, leading her to participate in community art projects or exhibitions that addressed themes of memory and remembrance.

Ultimately, Samuel's passing would have marked a turning point for Ella, infusing her work with new depth and meaning as she continued to explore the complexities of life, love, and loss through her art. The memories of her brother would linger in her heart and mind, serving as both an inspiration and a reminder of the enduring connections that shape our lives.

ELLA WAS 61 YEARS OLD when her father, Mordechai "Max," passed away in Kingston, Ontario, on December 27, 1980. His death marked another profound loss in her life, following the death of her brother just a few years prior. As a Hungarian Jew, Max likely had a rich history and cultural background that influenced his family's values and traditions. His passing would have deeply affected Ella, as she would have cherished the memories of her father's life, teachings, and the cultural heritage he passed down to her.

Growing up, Ella may have been shaped by her father's experiences and the stories he shared about his life in Hungary, his journey to Canada, and the challenges he faced as a Jewish immigrant. Max's resilience and strength could have inspired Ella's own artistic pursuits, fueling her desire to express herself and explore her identity through her art.

In the wake of his death, Ella might have found herself reflecting on the impact of her father's life on her own. She may have been reminded of the sacrifices he made for his family and the importance of preserving their Jewish heritage. This period could have prompted her to create artwork that honored his memory, perhaps exploring themes of family, identity, and the immigrant experience.

As she mourned, Ella might have sought solace in her community, connecting with other Jewish families and friends who understood her loss. Attending shiva and participating in other mourning rituals would have provided her with a sense of support and shared experience, allowing her to process her grief alongside those who loved her father.

In addition to her personal reflections, Ella may have considered how her father's legacy could be celebrated and remembered. She might have been inspired to create pieces that captured the essence of his character and values, infusing her work with the love and lessons he imparted. Whether through portraits, abstract pieces, or community art projects, her father's influence could have played a significant role in shaping the themes and emotions expressed in her art during this time.

Mordechai's passing would have underscored the fragility of life and the importance of familial bonds, prompting Ella to appreciate the relationships she still held dear. Through her art, she could have found a way to communicate her grief, honor her father's memory, and celebrate the rich tapestry of her family's history, ensuring that the legacy of Max and the values he instilled lived on through her work and the lives of future generations.

AT 62 YEARS OLD, IN 1981, Ella Marcus witnessed the introduction of compact discs (CDs), a technological innovation that would revolutionize the music industry and change the way art was consumed. This shift from vinyl records and cassette tapes to digital formats symbolized a broader transition towards modernity and accessibility in the arts.

For Ella, a passionate artist, this new medium may have sparked inspiration, influencing her creative process or how she perceived the relationship between art and technology. As the world embraced this digital revolution, artists began exploring new ways to incorporate technology into their work. Ella might have experimented with audio-visual art, combining her traditional painting techniques with sound, as the accessibility of music through CDs allowed for richer storytelling and emotional expression.

The 1980s were marked by a flourishing of various artistic movements, including postmodernism, which challenged traditional notions of art and embraced new media. Ella could have engaged with these trends, possibly participating in exhibitions that highlighted innovative practices. As she explored these changes, her work could have reflected her response to the cultural shifts occurring around her, contributing to the evolving dialogue in the art community.

This era also saw a growing recognition of women in the arts, with more opportunities for female artists to showcase their talents. Ella, having established her career earlier, might have served as a mentor to younger artists, sharing her experiences and encouraging the next generation to embrace their creativity amid the changing landscape.

Overall, the introduction of CDs not only marked a technological milestone but also represented a period of exploration and growth for Ella Marcus, both personally and artistically, as she navigated the exciting intersection of art and technology.

ELLA WAS 62 YEARS OLD when the Canada Act was passed on April 17, 1982. This significant piece of legislation, which patriated the Canadian Constitution and included the Charter of Rights and Freedoms, marked a pivotal moment in Canadian history. For Ella, who had experienced so many changes throughout her life, the passage of the Canada Act may have stirred a deep sense of national pride and hope for the future.

The Canada Act symbolized a shift towards greater autonomy for Canada, removing the last legal ties to the British Parliament. It established the constitutional framework that would protect the rights and freedoms of all Canadians, including the cultural rights of minority groups such as Jews. As an artist and a member of the Jewish community, Ella likely felt a renewed sense of belonging and recognition within the fabric of Canadian society. This change would resonate with her personal experiences as an immigrant's daughter, reinforcing her connection to the diverse mosaic of Canadian identity.

In the wake of the Canada Act, Ella may have felt inspired to reflect on her own identity as a Jewish woman in Canada and the importance of cultural expression. The inclusion of minority rights in the Charter could have motivated her to create art that celebrated her heritage, showcasing the rich traditions and values that shaped her upbringing. Perhaps she began to incorporate symbols and themes from her Jewish faith into her work, exploring the intersection of her identity as an artist and as a member of a minority community in Canada.

Ella's creative process during this period may have also been influenced by the broader socio-political climate in Canada. The Canada Act prompted conversations about rights, freedoms, and the recognition of diverse cultures within the country. As an artist, she might have felt a responsibility to engage with these themes, using her art as a platform to address social issues and promote understanding among different cultural groups. This could have led to collaborations with fellow artists from various backgrounds, fostering a sense of community and solidarity in their shared experiences.

In a world undergoing transformation, Ella's art may have reflected both her personal journey and the collective aspirations of a nation striving for equality and recognition. The Canada Act would likely serve as a backdrop for her artistic exploration, compelling her to consider the role of art in advocating for social justice and celebrating diversity. Ultimately, this landmark moment in Canadian history may have fueled Ella's passion for creating art that resonated with the evolving narrative of Canada—a narrative that embraced her own Jewish roots and honored the contributions of all Canadians to the rich tapestry of their shared identity.

ELLA MARCUS PASSED away at the age of 63 on January 12, 1983. Her death marked the end of a vibrant life filled with artistic expression and contributions to the creative community. As a Jew and an artist, her legacy likely resonated within her local community, particularly in Kingston, Ontario, where she is buried in Beth Israel Cemetery.

Her passing left a void not only in the lives of her family and friends but also in the artistic circles she had influenced. Throughout her life, Ella had embraced the evolving landscape of art and technology, and her work may have inspired many budding artists to explore new mediums and techniques. Even in her absence, her spirit and creativity likely continued to inspire others, reminding them of the importance of artistic expression and the impact one individual can have on a community.

As a testament to her life, those who visit her grave may reflect on her contributions to the art world and remember her as a passionate creator who dedicated her life to her craft, enriching the cultural tapestry of Kingston and beyond. Ella's legacy is preserved not only in her artwork but also in the hearts of those she touched during her lifetime.

Leah Miriam (Urtick) Marcus[10]

Leah Miriam nee Urtick was born in Romania in 1897, a time marked by significant political and social changes in Europe. Romania, situated at the crossroads of various cultures and empires, was experiencing a complex blend of modernization and tradition. The late 19th and early 20th centuries were characterized by the rise of nationalism, as various ethnic groups sought to assert their identities amidst the diverse tapestry of the region.

In Leah's early years, Romania was still part of the Austro-Hungarian Empire, which controlled much of Transylvania, a region that would have a profound influence on her life. The empire was a melting pot of cultures, with a substantial Jewish population that played a vital role in commerce, education, and the arts. For Jewish families like Leah's, life was often marked by a dual existence, balancing their cultural and religious identity with the pressures of integration into broader society.

Education for girls during this time was limited, but there was a growing movement advocating for women's rights and education, spurred by broader social changes across Europe. As a young girl, Leah would have faced challenges in accessing education, as traditional roles often confined women to domestic spheres. However, with the influence of progressive movements, some Jewish families prioritized education, leading to greater opportunities for their daughters.

The turn of the century brought significant social upheaval, including economic struggles and political instability. The labor movement was gaining traction, and protests were common as workers sought better conditions. For Leah's family, these changing dynamics may have spurred conversations about the future and the importance of resilience in the face of adversity.

━━━━━

LEAH'S BROTHER, JOSEPH, was born in Bacau, Romania, on July 10, 1897. Growing up in the same era as Leah, Joseph experienced the same cultural and social dynamics that characterized Jewish life in Romania during the late 19th and early 20th centuries. Bacau, a city known for its diverse population, would have provided Joseph with a rich tapestry of experiences as he navigated life in a multicultural environment.

The Urtig family, like many Jewish families of the time, faced the challenges and opportunities that came with their heritage. The decision to change the family surname to Urtick—except for Joseph, who chose to retain the original Urtig—reflects a common desire among immigrants and families in diaspora to adapt to their new surroundings while maintaining ties to their roots. This change could symbolize a quest for integration into the broader society while still honoring their Jewish identity.

As a young man, Joseph likely witnessed significant events that shaped his perspective and influenced his decisions. The political landscape in Romania was complex, marked by shifts in power, rising nationalism, and social movements that sought to improve the lives of marginalized groups, including Jews. Like many Jewish youths of his time, Joseph may have been active in community organizations or educational institutions that aimed to foster a sense of identity and solidarity among Jewish individuals.

The Urtig family's experiences during this period were undoubtedly shaped by the larger historical context. The aftermath of World War I and the subsequent social upheavals led to both challenges and opportunities for Jewish communities. Joseph's upbringing in this dynamic environment likely instilled in him a strong sense of resilience and an appreciation for the importance of family and community.

While Leah pursued her path, possibly focusing on education and the arts, Joseph may have developed different interests that reflected the opportunities and challenges of his time. The decision to retain the Urtig surname might indicate a strong attachment to his heritage and a desire to honor the family legacy amidst changing social dynamics.

As Joseph transitioned into adulthood, he would have faced a world in flux. The 1920s brought a mix of hope and uncertainty, as Romania experienced both cultural resurgence and rising anti-Semitism. Joseph's navigation of these complexities would have informed his perspective on identity, belonging, and the importance of maintaining cultural traditions in the face of external pressures.

Ultimately, Joseph's life, like Leah's, would be marked by the intricate balance of embracing new opportunities while holding fast to familial ties and cultural heritage. Their stories reflect the broader narrative of the Jewish experience in Romania, characterized by resilience, adaptation, and the enduring strength of community bonds. Joseph and Leah's journeys would intertwine, as their family dynamics and choices would shape their individual paths as they transitioned to life in Canada.

LEAH WAS FOUR YEARS old when her sister, Bella, was born in Bacau in 1901. Growing up in a close-knit Jewish family, Leah likely experienced a blend of joy and responsibility as she welcomed her new sibling into the world. The arrival of Bella not only expanded the family but also marked the beginning of Leah's role as an older sister, which would influence her upbringing and character.

In the early 1900s, Jewish families in Romania, particularly in towns like Bacau, often faced various challenges, including economic hardships and societal pressures. Leah's family would have needed to navigate these issues while instilling a sense of identity and tradition in their children. As Leah grew older, she would play a crucial role in helping to care for Bella and support her family, particularly in the context of a society that often marginalized Jewish communities.

The bond between Leah and Bella would have been significant, shaped by shared experiences, cultural practices, and familial responsibilities. As they both grew, Leah might have taken on the role of mentor and protector, teaching Bella about their heritage, values, and the importance of community.

By the time Leah reached her teenage years, she would have been navigating the complexities of young adulthood while also helping to raise Bella. This experience could have fostered a deep sense of empathy and understanding in Leah, shaping her character as a nurturing and supportive individual.

As the sisters matured, their lives would be interwoven with the broader historical and social changes occurring in Romania and Europe. The early 20th century brought significant transformations, including the effects of World War I and the emergence of new social movements. Leah's family, like many others, would need to adapt to these changes while maintaining their cultural identity.

Bella, growing up in the same environment as Leah, would have been influenced by her sister's guidance and the family's values. The sisterly bond could have provided both support and inspiration, as they faced the challenges of their time together.

The sisters' experiences would ultimately shape their perspectives on family, community, and identity, laying the foundation for their future journeys as they transitioned from Romania to life in Canada. The strength of their sisterly relationship would carry on as they faced the opportunities and challenges of immigrant life, marking an essential chapter in their family's narrative.

LEAH WAS SIX YEARS old when the first powered flight was made by the Wright brothers in 1903. This groundbreaking achievement marked a significant milestone in human history, capturing the imaginations of people around the world, including Leah and her family. As a young girl, she would have been filled with wonder at the idea of flight, dreaming of the possibilities that such innovation could bring.

In the backdrop of her childhood in Bacau, the world was undergoing rapid changes. The early 1900s were a time of industrial progress, and the thrill of technological advancements was palpable. While her family faced the everyday challenges of life, including economic pressures and the realities of being part of a marginalized Jewish community, the stories of the Wright brothers' success would have sparked hope and curiosity in young Leah.

As she observed the excitement surrounding flight, Leah might have been inspired by the notion that anything was possible through determination and innovation. This spirit could have influenced her ambitions and outlook on life. The early aviation feats also opened up discussions about exploration and the idea of connecting distant lands, perhaps even fueling Leah's family's aspirations for a better life beyond Romania.

Growing up during this transformative era, Leah would witness the world around her becoming increasingly interconnected. The innovations in transportation, including flight, would eventually play a crucial role in the migration patterns of many, including Jews fleeing persecution in Europe. For Leah's family, the dream of a brighter future could have started taking shape against this backdrop of rapid change.

The excitement of powered flight would resonate beyond just technological marvels; it represented hope and the pursuit of freedom. As Leah approached her adolescence, this sense of possibility would continue to shape her worldview, preparing her for the journeys and challenges that lay ahead in her life, including the eventual move to Canada where her own story would unfold against a new horizon.

LEAH WAS ELEVEN YEARS old when her sister, Bessie, was born in Romania in 1908. The arrival of a new sibling brought a mix of excitement and responsibility to Leah's life. As the eldest daughter in the family, Leah would have taken on a nurturing role, helping her mother care for Bessie and participating in the everyday tasks of raising a young child.

In the context of their family's Jewish heritage, Leah's role would have been significant. The bond between sisters was cherished, and Leah likely felt a deep sense of duty to protect and guide Bessie as they both navigated the complexities of life in their tight-knit community. Bessie's birth also represented a moment of joy amidst the challenges their family faced, including social and economic struggles that were common for Jewish families in Eastern Europe at that time.

By 1908, Romania was experiencing political and social changes, including growing tensions related to minority rights. Leah's family, being Jewish, may have faced discrimination, and the arrival of Bessie would have added both to their joys and concerns about the future. Leah would have grown increasingly aware of the external pressures on their family and community, fostering a sense of resilience and determination within her.

As Leah transitioned into her teenage years, she would have been influenced not just by the dynamics of her family life but also by the broader cultural shifts occurring around her. The early 20th century was marked by movements advocating for rights and opportunities, which could have inspired Leah as she observed the world changing.

With Bessie by her side, Leah would come to understand the importance of sisterhood and familial bonds, finding strength in their relationship as they faced the uncertainties of their environment. This nurturing spirit and sense of responsibility would remain with Leah throughout her life, shaping her into a supportive figure for those around her as she would later carve out her own path in a new country.

LEAH WAS THIRTEEN YEARS old when her brother Abraham, affectionately known as "Al," was born in Bacău on April 13, 1910. The arrival of Al marked another joyful milestone for Leah and her family, adding a new layer of warmth and complexity to their household. As a teenager, Leah would have been acutely aware of her responsibilities growing within the family dynamic, now taking on the role of a protective older sister alongside her nurturing instincts for her younger siblings, Bella and Bessie.

With Al's birth, Leah likely felt a deepening sense of familial duty, as her parents would have relied on her to help care for him while balancing her own adolescence. The bond between siblings was especially significant in their Jewish culture, and Leah would have taken pride in introducing Al to family traditions, stories, and the values that shaped their identities.

By 1910, Romania was navigating its own social and political challenges. The Jewish community was often caught in the crosscurrents of nationalism and rising anti-Semitism. As a young girl, Leah would have been beginning to understand these complexities while also experiencing the joys of childhood. Having a new brother in the family could have been a source of comfort amid the societal uncertainties surrounding them.

Leah, now a young woman, would have been excited to guide All through the early years of his life, instilling in him a sense of pride in their heritage and the importance of community. This nurturing relationship would serve not only to strengthen their sibling bond but also to equip Al with the resilience needed to navigate the world they inhabited.

As she transitioned into her late teens, Leah's protective instincts for Al would have only grown stronger. She would have had a keen awareness of the challenges their family faced, especially as their lives unfolded against the backdrop of changing societal conditions in Romania. Leah's experiences during these formative years, filled with moments of joy and challenges, would help mold her into a steadfast pillar of support for her siblings, fostering a close-knit family unit in times of both happiness and hardship.

LEAH MARRIED MORDECHAI Marcus, a significant event that marked a new chapter in her life. Their union brought together two families, combining their heritage and traditions, as they both came from Jewish backgrounds. Leah, with her nurturing spirit and strong familial bonds, likely approached marriage with a sense of commitment to building a life filled with love, support, and community values.

Mordechai, a Hungarian Jew, would have brought his own experiences and cultural influences into the marriage. Together, they would have created a home that reflected their shared beliefs, traditions, and aspirations. This partnership likely focused on fostering a strong Jewish identity for their future children and instilling in them the importance of family ties, cultural heritage, and resilience in the face of challenges.

As they settled into married life, Leah and Mordechai would have faced the realities of their time, including the economic conditions and political atmosphere in Canada after their immigration. Their shared experiences and mutual support would have been crucial as they navigated the complexities of raising a family and establishing their place in a new country.

Throughout their marriage, Leah and Mordechai would have celebrated Jewish holidays, participated in community events, and upheld traditions that were essential to their identity. This emphasis on cultural heritage would have been a cornerstone of their family life, creating a nurturing environment for their children to grow and thrive.

Leah's caring nature, combined with Mordechai's influence, would have shaped their family dynamics, fostering a deep sense of belonging and community among their children. Their marriage would be characterized by mutual respect, shared responsibilities, and a commitment to building a loving home where traditions were cherished and the values of compassion and resilience were instilled in the next generation.

____

AT THE AGE OF 22, LEAH welcomed her daughter Ella into the world on June 5, 1919. This was a momentous occasion that would forever change the course of Leah's life. Ella's birth brought joy and fulfillment to Leah as she embraced her role as a mother, nurturing her child with love and dedication.

As a young mother, Leah was likely eager to impart her values, traditions, and cultural heritage to Ella. She would have shared stories of their family's history, emphasizing the importance of their Jewish identity and the customs they held dear. Leah's nurturing spirit would have created a warm and loving environment, where Ella could grow and thrive, surrounded by the support of her family.

Ella's arrival also meant that Leah had to navigate the challenges of motherhood during a time of social and economic change. The early 20th century was marked by significant events, including the aftermath of World War I and the beginning of social reforms. Leah would have been aware of the shifting dynamics in society, and her experiences as an immigrant would have influenced how she raised Ella.

As Ella grew, Leah would have celebrated milestones with her, from her first steps to her first words, all while instilling a sense of resilience and determination. She likely encouraged Ella's creativity and aspirations, fostering a love of learning and exploration. Their bond would have been strengthened by shared moments of joy, laughter, and the challenges of everyday life.

In this nurturing environment, Ella would have developed a strong sense of self and a deep appreciation for her family's roots. Leah's guidance and support would have played a crucial role in shaping Ella's character and values, preparing her for the journey ahead as she grew into a remarkable woman in her own right.

AT THE AGE OF 28, LEAH welcomed her son, Samuel David Marcus, into the world on September 18, 1925. The birth of Samuel marked another significant milestone in Leah's life, further enriching her role as a mother and expanding her family's legacy.

As Samuel grew, Leah embraced her responsibilities with love and devotion, nurturing his development and instilling the values that she held dear. She likely encouraged his curiosity about the world, fostering an environment where he felt safe to explore and learn. Leah's experiences as an immigrant and her Jewish heritage would have profoundly influenced the lessons she imparted to Samuel, ensuring he understood the importance of family, tradition, and resilience.

Leah may have shared stories from her own childhood, connecting Samuel to their family's history and heritage. She probably emphasized the significance of community, teaching him about the importance of supporting one another and being part of something larger than oneself. Through holidays, family gatherings, and rituals, Leah helped Samuel develop a sense of belonging to both his immediate family and the wider Jewish community.

As a young boy, Samuel would have experienced the world through Leah's loving guidance, celebrating his milestones with the same enthusiasm and warmth that marked Ella's upbringing. From his first steps to learning how to read, each achievement would have been a cause for celebration. Leah's nurturing spirit and unwavering support would have provided Samuel with a strong foundation, helping him grow into a confident and compassionate individual.

Leah's dedication to her children reflected her commitment to ensuring that they thrived in a world that was often challenging and unpredictable. As the family continued to grow, Leah remained a pillar of strength and love, navigating the joys and challenges of motherhood with grace. Samuel's birth added to the tapestry of her life, weaving in new experiences and memories that would shape their family's future.

AT THE AGE OF 39, LEAH experienced the profound loss of her mother, Anna (née Pollack), who passed away in Montreal, Quebec, on October 3, 1936. The death of a parent is often a pivotal moment in one's life, and for Leah, this loss would have marked a significant emotional transition.

Anna's passing likely left Leah reflecting on her own experiences as a daughter and mother. She may have recalled the lessons and values imparted by her mother, the traditions they shared, and the strength Anna exhibited throughout her life. In times of grief, these memories can be a source of comfort, helping Leah navigate her own journey of motherhood while honoring her mother's legacy.

As a Jewish woman in the 1930s, Leah might have found solace in her community and faith during this difficult time. The rituals surrounding mourning in Jewish tradition, such as sitting shiva, would have allowed her family and friends to come together in support, sharing their own memories of Anna and celebrating her life. Leah likely drew strength from this communal support, reaffirming the bonds that connected her to her heritage and family.

Following Anna's death, Leah would have continued to nurture her children, Ella and Samuel, instilling in them the values she learned from her mother. She might have encouraged them to remember their grandmother through stories and traditions, ensuring that Anna's spirit lived on in their lives. This connection to their ancestry would have provided Leah's children with a sense of identity and belonging, even in the face of loss.

Despite the sorrow of losing her mother, Leah's resilience would have been essential in guiding her family through the grieving process. As she coped with her own emotions, she would have remained committed to providing a loving and supportive environment for Ella and Samuel, demonstrating the strength that characterized both her and her mother. Through this journey, Leah continued to honor Anna's memory by embodying the love, compassion, and tenacity that defined their family.

JUST A FEW WEEKS AFTER the death of her mother, Leah faced an even greater sorrow with the passing of her father, Isaac, in Montreal on October 29, 1936. The loss of both parents in such a short span of time would have been devastating for Leah, leaving her to grapple with the overwhelming grief and emotional void left by their absence.

At the age of 39, Leah was now faced with the reality of navigating her life as an adult orphan. The dual loss would have deepened her sense of responsibility toward her own children, Ella and Samuel. Leah likely felt compelled to ensure that her children understood the importance of family and heritage, instilling in them the values her parents had passed down.

Isaac's death would have prompted Leah to reflect on her upbringing and the lessons imparted by both of her parents. As a Jewish family, they would have celebrated traditions and rituals that provided a framework for their lives. Leah might have leaned into these customs as a source of comfort during this turbulent time, seeking solace in her community and faith.

The grieving period for both parents would have been filled with rituals in accordance with Jewish customs, including mourning practices such as sitting shiva. This time would have allowed Leah and her family to come together in shared remembrance, honoring the lives of Isaac and Anna while supporting one another through their collective grief.

With the loss of her parents, Leah would have likely taken on a more significant role in her family's legacy, emphasizing the importance of remembering and celebrating the lives of those who came before them. She might have shared stories of her parents with Ella and Samuel, ensuring that their memories were preserved and cherished.

As she navigated her own sorrow, Leah would also have felt a profound need to create a stable and loving environment for her children. The dual losses would have further strengthened her resolve to honor her parents by fostering a close-knit family dynamic, drawing on the love and values she learned throughout her life. Through resilience and determination, Leah aimed to keep the spirit of her parents alive in the hearts of her children, instilling in them a sense of pride in their heritage and the importance of family bonds.

AT THE AGE OF 42, LEAH witnessed Canada joining the global effort as it entered into World War II in 1939. The war marked a period of profound uncertainty, sacrifice, and change, deeply affecting Jewish communities around the world. For Leah, it brought not only the anxiety of the war itself but a personal worry when her brother Joseph, living in the United States, was drafted to serve.

Knowing that Joseph was actively involved in the war would have filled Leah with both pride and fear. As a sister, she would have held memories of their shared childhood in Romania close to her heart, along with the protective instinct that often comes with being the older sibling. Her thoughts would frequently turn to him, hoping for his safe return and praying for his well-being.

Joseph's service would have also sparked a sense of admiration within the family, as he represented their resilience and commitment to supporting those in need, embodying the values that had been instilled in them by their parents, Anna and Isaac. The war years were challenging, with families separated and many enduring hardship, but the community around Leah also found strength in coming together.

Leah would have felt a renewed responsibility to instill strength and resilience in her children, Ella and Samuel, knowing the uncertainty of the world they were growing up in. She would have encouraged them to appreciate each day and reminded them of their family's strength and adaptability. The unity and support of her community would have been a valuable resource for Leah during this time, offering solace and solidarity as they shared similar fears and challenges brought about by the war.

As news of battles and distant conflicts reached her, Leah focused on keeping her household stable and nurturing her children's understanding of resilience and unity. For Leah, knowing that her brother was among those fighting likely inspired her to emphasize the importance of family, heritage, and courage. Through these challenging years, Leah managed her worry for Joseph and her desire to maintain a nurturing environment for her family. Her enduring strength became a lasting example for Ella and Samuel, showing them how to face adversity with dignity, resilience, and hope.

AS AN ACTIVE MEMBER of the Beth Israel synagogue and the secretary of the Queen Esther Hadassah Chapter, Leah's life was intertwined with her community. Her involvement in these organizations wasn't just a role; it was a testament to her commitment to her faith, culture, and the well-being of the Jewish community in her city. In Beth Israel, Leah found not only a place of worship but a second family, offering her support and camaraderie.

Serving as the secretary of the Queen Esther Hadassah Chapter highlighted Leah's dedication to philanthropy and community leadership. The Hadassah organization, known for its emphasis on health, education, and support for Israel, was a cause Leah believed deeply in. Her role likely involved coordinating meetings, organizing events, and connecting with members to fundraise and advocate for humanitarian needs both locally and abroad. Leah's commitment to her role was a source of pride, as she knew her work was contributing to causes close to her heart and to the preservation of Jewish culture and welfare.

Through her work with Hadassah, Leah became a mentor and a pillar within her community. She represented strength and reliability, qualities that inspired other women to step forward in service. Her activities kept her closely connected with like-minded women, fostering a network of friendship and support, while also giving her a meaningful way to give back to her community.

In her synagogue and community work, Leah would have instilled a sense of pride and cultural identity in her children, Ella and Samuel, passing on her values of generosity, resilience, and active faith. Her leadership, both in her household and the community, left a legacy of compassion and dedication, qualities she hoped her children would carry forward into their own lives.

—————

IN ADDITION TO HER roles within the Beth Israel synagogue and the Queen Esther Hadassah Chapter, Leah was also a dedicated member of the Sisterhood Auxiliary. The Sisterhood Auxiliary provided a support network for the synagogue's activities and played a crucial role in fostering a close-knit community, especially among the women who managed family life, community service, and faith-based obligations.

Leah's involvement in the Sisterhood Auxiliary added another layer to her community service, enabling her to contribute to various events, fundraisers, and outreach programs. Through the Auxiliary, she helped organize holiday gatherings, educational programs, and charitable drives, extending her synagogue's support to those in need and strengthening the bonds among community members. Her role in the Auxiliary allowed her to engage in hands-on work, where her administrative skills, warmth, and dedication made a significant difference.

This engagement provided her with meaningful connections, creating friendships that enriched her personal life and support during both joyful and challenging times. Through the Sisterhood Auxiliary, Leah could share her values and mentor younger women, passing down the importance of community service, cultural pride, and mutual support. In her children's eyes, Leah's dedication to these roles reinforced a sense of duty, generosity, and faith, and they likely viewed her as a source of inspiration and wisdom within their family and beyond.

BY THE TIME OF HER passing, Leah had also served as a member of the Central Home and School Board, reflecting her dedication to the educational environment in her community. Her involvement with the board would have allowed her to advocate for the needs and interests of students, parents, and educators, shaping school programs and initiatives that directly impacted the quality of education in Kingston.

Leah's passing on July 28, 1941, at the age of 44, took place at Hotel Dieu Hospital in Kingston, following an operation. Her untimely death left a void in her family and among those who had come to rely on her guidance, kindness, and community spirit. Leah's legacy was one of resilience and commitment to her faith, her family, and her community. She was laid to rest with dignity, and her contributions to various social, educational, and religious causes continued to be remembered by those whose lives she touched. Her family and community held onto her memory as a model of selfless service and dedication to the well-being of others.

Mordechai "Max" Marcus[11]

In 1898, Romania was a predominantly rural country, and life for many Jews there was challenging. While Romania had gained independence two decades earlier in 1878, Jewish residents often faced widespread discrimination and limitations on their rights. Many Jews in Romania struggled with social restrictions, economic hardships, and limited access to opportunities, which were compounded by restrictive laws that marginalized them.

The Romanian economy at the time relied heavily on agriculture, and opportunities for urban growth were scarce, especially for Jewish families. Jews were often restricted from owning land or entering certain professions. As a result, many Jewish communities turned to trades, crafts, or small businesses in urban areas, building tightly-knit communities in cities like Bacau.

Despite these hardships, Jewish communities maintained a strong cultural identity. Synagogues and community organizations were central to Jewish life, providing spiritual support, cultural continuity, and a sense of resilience in the face of adversity. In 1898, Mordechai "Max" Marcus's birth would have been marked with hopes for a better future, though his family likely experienced the constraints and challenges typical for Jews in Romania at the time.

MORDECHAI "MAX" MARCUS was just 4 years old in 1903 when the Wright brothers achieved the first powered flight at Kitty Hawk, North Carolina. This event marked a groundbreaking moment in history, symbolizing the beginning of human exploration of the skies.

For the Jewish communities of Romania, however, daily life remained largely unaffected by these technological advancements, as they continued to focus on preserving their traditions and supporting their families amid societal constraints.

Though still very young, Max would grow up in a world where new inventions and ideas were rapidly transforming everyday life globally, even if these changes reached Romania slowly. The significance of this first flight would later influence many industries and ways of life, including communication, travel, and warfare, setting the stage for the more interconnected world Max would come to experience as he grew older.

AT 20 YEARS OLD, MAX Marcus became a father when his daughter Ella was born on June 5, 1919. This was an era marked by both celebration and transformation. World War I had recently ended, and Romania, like much of Europe, was experiencing significant political and social changes. With the formation of Greater Romania in 1918, the country expanded its borders, bringing together diverse ethnic and religious groups under one government.

For Jewish families like the Marcuses, life in Romania was a mix of new opportunities and ongoing challenges. While some areas saw increased tolerance and inclusion, others remained deeply affected by discrimination and restrictions on Jewish rights. Max and his family likely balanced these realities as he worked to provide stability for his young family.

The arrival of Ella represented hope and continuity in a world that was rapidly changing. She was born into a family rooted in tradition yet surrounded by the early stages of the modern era.

AT 26, MAX MARCUS FACED the loss of his father, Isaac, who passed away on November 22, 1924, in Montreal. The event would have been a significant turning point in his life, as the death of a parent often shifted family dynamics and responsibilities. Max was in the early stages of adulthood, and this loss may have added both emotional weight and new responsibilities as he continued to support his young family and manage his obligations.

The year 1924 also marked a period of growth and change for Jewish communities in Canada. Montreal's Jewish population was expanding, and many Jewish immigrants and their families were establishing roots in cities like Montreal and Kingston. While Canada provided more stability than Eastern Europe, Jewish families still faced challenges in overcoming prejudice and adapting to new societal norms.

———————

AT 27, MAX MARCUS WELCOMED the birth of his son, Samuel David, on September 18, 1925. This would have been a time of joy and responsibility for Max, as his family grew during a period of change and modernization in Canada. The mid-1920s saw Canadian society shifting toward urbanization and a more industrialized economy, which affected communities across the country, including those in Kingston and Montreal.

As a Jewish father, Max would have been focused on providing for his family while instilling cultural and religious values, despite the challenges Jewish communities often faced. Jewish families like the Marcuses maintained their traditions through close-knit community networks, participation in synagogues, and involvement in local Jewish organizations that provided support and a sense of identity.

———————

AT 33, MAX MARCUS WAS living in Canada when Stalin's Great Terror began in the Soviet Union. This campaign of intense political repression, which began in the late 1930s, was marked by mass arrests, forced labor camps, and widespread executions. News of Stalin's actions would have reached Canada, influencing political discussions and intensifying debates about authoritarianism, communism, and democracy.

For many Jewish immigrants from Eastern Europe, like Max, Stalin's reign of terror brought a mix of concern and caution, as it impacted the Jewish communities in Soviet-controlled regions. Families with relatives still in Europe or in communist territories may have felt a sense of dread, knowing that their loved ones were at risk of persecution, especially during a time when authoritarian regimes were on the rise.

HE WAS 42 YEARS OLD when his wife, Leah, passed away in Kingston, Ontario, on July 28, 1941. Her death marked a significant emotional loss for him, especially considering their shared life and family. Just a few weeks later, on October 29, 1941, he lost his father, Isaac, which compounded his grief.

During this time, Max faced the challenges of raising their children, Ella and Samuel David, while dealing with the profound sorrow of losing his wife. He continued to be active in his community and at the Beth Israel synagogue, providing support to his family and others in need during the war years.

Max lived through the tumultuous period of World War II, witnessing the global impacts of the conflict and the experiences of those around him. He remained a dedicated father and community member, navigating life as a widower while fostering resilience in the face of adversity.

———————

HE WAS 50 YEARS OLD when Canada became a founding member of NATO on April 4, 1949. This marked a significant moment in Canadian history as the country committed to collective defense in the face of global tensions during the Cold War. For Max, a Jew who had experienced the upheaval of both world wars and the broader geopolitical shifts of the 20th century, this development likely resonated deeply.

As a member of a community with a history of seeking safety and security, Max may have viewed NATO's formation as a hopeful step toward international cooperation and peace. He continued to raise his children, Ella and Samuel David, instilling in them the values of community engagement and responsibility.

Throughout the 1950s, Max would have observed Canada growing in its role on the world stage, navigating relationships with both its allies and adversaries. This period was characterized by significant social changes and economic development, as Canada increasingly defined its national identity amid global shifts.

Max remained involved in his local community, supporting initiatives that benefited Jewish life in Kingston and beyond, all while reflecting on the tumultuous events of his past and the future of his children in a rapidly changing world.

———————

HE WAS 56 YEARS OLD when his sister, Mary, passed away in Montreal on November 14, 1954. Her death marked another poignant moment in Max's life, as he mourned the loss of a sibling with whom he likely shared a deep bond. Growing up in Romania and later settling in Canada, their shared experiences would have fostered a unique understanding between them, encompassing the challenges of immigration, the impact of war, and the quest for a stable life in a new country.

Mary's passing may have brought back memories of their childhood in Romania, the family gatherings, and the struggles they faced as Jews in a changing world. For Max, who had already faced the loss of his wife Leah thirteen years prior, this event could have deepened his sense of solitude and the need for familial connections.

In the following years, Max continued to navigate life in Kingston, raising his children, Ella and Samuel David. He likely drew strength from his community ties, participating in Jewish life in Kingston and remaining active in local organizations. The experience of loss would have underscored the importance of family and community for him, as he sought to create a supportive environment for his children amidst the changes around them.

As he aged, Max also witnessed significant developments in Canadian society, including advancements in civil rights and growing multiculturalism, reflecting on how these shifts influenced the Jewish community and his family's place within it. His resilience and commitment to his heritage became more crucial as he sought to instill those values in his children during a time of societal transformation.

HE WAS 61 YEARS OLD when Canada introduced its first Bill of Rights on August 10, 1960. This landmark legislation aimed to protect the rights and freedoms of Canadians and was a significant step toward establishing a more inclusive society. For Max, a Jewish immigrant who had experienced the challenges of discrimination and the importance of civil liberties, this development likely held great significance.

The introduction of the Bill of Rights may have provided Max with a renewed sense of hope for a future where individual rights were recognized and protected, especially for minority communities like his own. He might have seen it as an opportunity for greater acceptance and integration within Canadian society, reflecting on his family's journey from Romania to Canada and the challenges they faced along the way.

In his community, Max could have participated in discussions about the implications of this new legislation, sharing his experiences and insights with others. He may have felt a sense of responsibility to ensure that his children, Ella and Samuel David, understood the importance of standing up for their rights and the rights of others.

As the 1960s progressed, Max continued to witness significant social changes, including movements for civil rights and equality across North America. These developments likely influenced his perspectives on community engagement and advocacy, reinforcing the values of justice and solidarity that he wanted to impart to his family.

Max's life during this time would have been characterized by a deepening connection to both his Jewish heritage and his Canadian identity, as he navigated the complexities of raising a family in a society increasingly focused on human rights and social justice.

HE WAS 63 YEARS OLD when Saskatchewan Medicare was implemented in 1962, serving as a pioneering model for universal healthcare in Canada. This program, established by Premier Tommy Douglas, marked a significant shift in how healthcare was provided across the country and laid the groundwork for the Canada Health Act of 1984.

For Max, who had lived through various healthcare systems and witnessed the challenges faced by those without access to adequate medical care, the establishment of Medicare likely represented a profound milestone. He may have appreciated the importance of ensuring that all Canadians, regardless of their financial means, had the right to receive necessary medical treatment.

In the Jewish community, healthcare access was particularly relevant, as many immigrants faced barriers due to language and cultural differences. Max might have been involved in discussions within his community about the implications of Medicare, recognizing its potential to improve the lives of families like his own.

Moreover, the introduction of Saskatchewan Medicare could have sparked conversations around the importance of collective responsibility and community support. Max likely felt a sense of pride that Canada was moving towards a more equitable healthcare system, aligning with his values of social justice and solidarity.

As he reflected on his family's experiences, Max might have considered how universal healthcare could positively impact the next generation, including his children, Ella and Samuel David. He may have hoped that they would live in a society that prioritized the well-being of all its members, fostering a greater sense of unity and compassion.

During this time, Max continued to engage with local community organizations and advocate for social issues that mattered to him, reinforcing the belief that everyone deserves access to quality healthcare. The establishment of Saskatchewan Medicare would have inspired him to remain active in his community, supporting initiatives that furthered the cause of social equity and welfare.

***

HE WAS 70 YEARS OLD when his brother, Jack, passed away in Montreal on December 5, 1968. The loss of Jack, who had likely been a significant presence in his life, would have deeply affected Max. They shared a bond that was rooted in their experiences as Jewish immigrants, navigating life's challenges together. Jack's passing marked the end of an era for Max, as he reflected on their shared childhood memories and the journeys they undertook as brothers.

At the time of Jack's death, Max was living in a world that was rapidly changing. The late 1960s were marked by social upheaval, civil rights movements, and a reevaluation of traditional values. Max may have found solace in the memories of their family and the importance of maintaining strong familial ties during such transformative times. He likely recalled their parents' sacrifices and the values instilled in them, which had shaped their paths.

As a member of the Jewish community in Montreal, Max might have participated in mourning rituals and gatherings to honor Jack's memory. These customs would have provided a sense of comfort and connection, reinforcing the importance of community during times of grief.

In his later years, Max may have taken on a more active role within the community, finding purpose in supporting those who had also experienced loss. He might have become involved in initiatives that provided assistance to families in mourning, drawing from his own experiences to help others navigate similar challenges.

Jack's passing may have also prompted Max to reflect on his own legacy and the values he wanted to impart to his children, Ella and Samuel David. He may have emphasized the importance of family bonds, resilience, and the need to support one another through life's difficulties.

Ultimately, Jack's death was a poignant reminder of the fragility of life, inspiring Max to cherish the moments he had left with his loved ones and to continue engaging with the community that had supported him throughout his journey.

HE WAS 75 YEARS OLD when his brother Philip passed away in Israel on January 9, 1974. The loss of Philip, who had likely settled in Israel after the Second World War, would have been particularly poignant for Max, especially considering the historical significance of Israel in their family's narrative and the deep connection many Jews feel towards the land.

Max, at 75, was navigating his twilight years amid significant global changes. The early 1970s were marked by political turmoil and conflict in the Middle East, including the aftermath of the Yom Kippur War, which took place later in 1973. News of Philip's death may have reached him during a time of heightened tension and uncertainty in Israel, adding to the emotional weight of the moment.

Philip's passing would have stirred memories of their childhood together, recalling the struggles they faced as immigrants and the dreams they held for a better life. It might have also prompted Max to reflect on the choices that led Philip to Israel, a place that symbolized hope and renewal for many Jews around the world. Max may have felt a mix of pride for Philip's contributions to the Israeli community and sorrow for the family connections that would now be more difficult to maintain.

In the wake of Philip's death, Max might have sought comfort within his own family, emphasizing the importance of maintaining strong ties with Ella and Samuel David. The family would likely have gathered to mourn Philip, sharing stories and memories that would help keep his spirit alive. Max might have encouraged his children to learn more about their heritage and the sacrifices made by their relatives, instilling a sense of pride and responsibility to honor those who had come before them.

As a member of the Jewish community, Max could have participated in memorial services or organized gatherings to commemorate Philip's life. These events would have reinforced the bonds of community, offering a space for collective mourning and shared memories.

Philip's death also served as a reminder for Max about the passage of time and the importance of cherishing the moments he had left. He may have taken this opportunity to reflect on his own legacy, focusing on the values he wished to impart to the next generation and the stories he wanted to share about their family history.

Overall, Philip's passing was a significant moment in Max's life, evoking a deep sense of loss while also reinforcing the importance of family, community, and cultural heritage in navigating the complexities of life.

HE WAS 76 YEARS OLD when his son Samuel David passed away in Kingston, Ontario, on January 30, 1975. The loss of a child is often one of the most devastating experiences a parent can endure, and for Max, this would have been an immeasurable grief.

Samuel, who had been born on September 18, 1925, likely had a rich life filled with his own struggles and triumphs. His passing may have been preceded by health issues, but regardless of the circumstances, it would have left a profound void in Max's life. At 76, Max was already facing the challenges of aging, and the death of his son would have compounded feelings of isolation and sorrow.

Max might have struggled with questions of legacy, reflecting on what he had imparted to Samuel and whether he had done enough as a father. The bond between father and son, shaped through years of shared experiences, was now severed, leaving Max with memories of better times. He may have found himself reminiscing about Samuel's childhood, the dreams he held, and the love that connected them.

The Jewish community in Kingston would likely have rallied around Max during this difficult time, offering support and sharing in his mourning. Jewish traditions surrounding death emphasize the importance of community, and the rituals associated with grieving—such as sitting shiva—would have provided Max with a structured way to process his grief. Friends and family would have come together to offer comfort, share stories of Samuel, and help Max navigate his sorrow.

As he mourned Samuel, Max may have also drawn strength from his daughter Ella and the remaining family members. Their presence would have been vital, reminding him that, despite the losses he faced, there was still love and support around him. Max might have encouraged them to carry forward Samuel's memory, urging them to remember the lessons and values he had instilled in them.

The grief of losing Samuel would likely have weighed heavily on Max's heart, yet it may also have sparked a desire to share their family history and stories more fervently. He could have felt an urgency to pass on the legacy of their family, ensuring that Samuel's contributions and spirit would live on in the hearts of his loved ones.

In the months following Samuel's passing, Max may have reflected on the importance of family and the bonds that held them together, as well as the fragility of life itself. This experience would serve as a poignant reminder for Max to cherish the time he had left with those he loved, fostering deeper connections and creating lasting memories in honor of his beloved son.

HE WAS 82 YEARS OLD when he passed away on December 27, 1980, in Kingston, Ontario. The end of his life marked the conclusion of a journey filled with personal and familial challenges, resilience, and the enduring impact of his Jewish heritage.

As Max approached his final years, he likely reflected on a lifetime rich with experiences, from his early years in Romania to his immigration to Canada and the various milestones he had witnessed along the way. At 82, he had lived through significant historical events, including two World Wars, the Holocaust, the establishment of the State of Israel, and major societal changes in Canada.

In Kingston, Max would have been surrounded by family, including his daughter Ella and her family, who likely remained close and supportive as he aged. His community, rooted in the Jewish faith, would have provided comfort and connection, reinforcing the values of family and tradition that were so important to him.

In his later years, Max might have enjoyed sharing stories of his past with his grandchildren, imparting wisdom and life lessons he had learned throughout his journey. He may have taken pride in their achievements and felt a sense of fulfillment in seeing the next generation thrive, carrying on the family legacy.

His death on December 27 would have been a time of profound grief for his family. Jewish mourning practices, such as sitting shiva, would have provided a structured way for his loved ones to grieve and honor his memory. Family and friends would gather to share stories, light candles, and remember the life he lived, emphasizing the importance of community support in times of loss.

Max's passing would also serve as a moment of reflection for those who knew him, reminding them of the fragility of life and the significance of familial bonds. His contributions to the Kingston community and the memories he created would continue to resonate long after he was gone.

Buried in Beth Israel Cemetery, Max's final resting place would serve as a testament to his life and faith. The cemetery, a place where many Jewish families found solace and connection, would provide a space for his descendants to visit, remember, and honor him.

In the years that followed, his family would likely continue to share stories about him, ensuring that his legacy lived on through their memories, traditions, and the values he had instilled in them. His life would remain an integral part of their family's narrative, a reminder of their roots and the enduring strength of their heritage.

Samuel David Marcus[12]

Samuel was born in Kingston, Ontario on September 18, 1925. In 1925, life was marked by significant changes and developments across various spheres, including politics, culture, and technology. Samuel David was born in Kingston, Ontario, during a time when the world was gradually recovering from the turmoil of World War I, and the Roaring Twenties was in full swing.

Economic Context

The mid-1920s were characterized by economic prosperity in many parts of the world, particularly in North America. The United States and Canada experienced growth, with rising consumerism and a flourishing middle class. Factories ramped up production, and the availability of new products and conveniences became more pronounced. However, this prosperity would soon be challenged by the Great Depression, which began in 1929.

Social Changes

The 1920s, often referred to as the Jazz Age, saw a shift in social norms and values. The decade was known for its cultural vibrancy, particularly in music and arts. Jazz music gained immense popularity, and the emergence of radio as a medium of entertainment brought music and news into homes across North America.

Women were also beginning to challenge traditional roles, with many advocating for suffrage and greater participation in public life. In Canada, women had gained the right to vote in federal elections in 1918, and by the mid-1920s, they were increasingly involved in various professions and social movements.

Technological Advancements

Technological innovations were transforming everyday life. The introduction of household appliances, such as electric refrigerators and washing machines, began to change domestic life, making tasks easier and freeing up time for leisure activities. The automobile became more accessible to the average family, contributing to greater mobility and the development of suburban areas.

Health and Education

Public health measures were also improving, leading to better overall health outcomes. Vaccines were becoming more common, and public health campaigns focused on sanitation and hygiene. Education was expanding, with an increasing emphasis on higher education and vocational training for young people.

Jewish Community

For Samuel David's family, as Jews in Canada, the 1920s represented a time of both opportunity and challenge. Many Jewish immigrants had settled in Canada, and communities were establishing synagogues, schools, and social organizations to support one another. Despite facing anti-Semitism and discrimination, the Jewish community was making strides in various fields, including business, arts, and politics.

Family Life

In Kingston, Ontario, Samuel David's family would have experienced the warmth of community and family ties. The social fabric of the city was likely woven with close-knit families, local traditions, and cultural practices that reinforced their Jewish identity. Family gatherings and celebrations would have been significant, emphasizing the importance of heritage and the passing down of traditions to the next generation.

In summary, Samuel David's birth in 1925 took place against a backdrop of economic growth, cultural vibrancy, and social change, setting the stage for his own life and the experiences he would navigate in the decades to come.

SAMUEL DAVID WAS SIX years old in 1931 when Joseph Stalin's regime in the Soviet Union began a period of intense political repression and state-sponsored terror, which had far-reaching consequences that extended beyond Soviet borders.

Context of Stalin's Terror

1. Political Repression: Stalin's rule was marked by the purging of perceived political enemies. The Great Purge (or Great Terror), which peaked in the late 1930s, involved widespread arrests, executions, and imprisonment in gulags. While this terror was primarily directed towards Soviet citizens, its repercussions affected many Jewish communities in Eastern Europe, leading to increased migration and a sense of insecurity among Jews worldwide.

---

2. FAMINE AND FORCED Collectivization: One of the most devastating impacts of Stalin's policies was the forced collectivization of agriculture, which aimed to consolidate individual landholdings into collective farms. This led to widespread famine, particularly in Ukraine, where millions perished in the Holodomor (1932-1933). This humanitarian disaster created a ripple effect, as families fled to escape the dire conditions.

---

3. GLOBAL JEWISH CONCERNS: The Jewish community globally was deeply affected by the political climate in the Soviet Union. Many Jews had hoped for better treatment under the Bolshevik regime following the Russian Revolution in 1917. However, the subsequent repression, especially against Jewish cultural and religious practices, fueled anxiety and uncertainty. This period marked a significant shift in Jewish diaspora politics, with many looking to emigrate to safer places like North America.

IMPACT ON SAMUEL DAVID and His Family

For Samuel David's family, living in Kingston, Ontario, during this time would have meant grappling with the news of terror unfolding across the ocean. Although they were safe in Canada, the effects of Stalin's reign of terror likely influenced their community dynamics and conversations about identity, safety, and belonging.

1. Community Response: Jewish communities in Canada often came together in solidarity, holding fundraisers, writing letters, and advocating for those affected by the terror in Eastern Europe. Samuel's family might have been involved in supporting Jewish refugees who fled the oppressive regime.

2. CULTURAL IDENTITY: The fear and suffering experienced by fellow Jews would have reinforced a collective cultural identity. Discussions about the importance of maintaining Jewish traditions and supporting each other through times of hardship would have been prevalent in homes and synagogues.

3. EDUCATION AND AWARENESS: As Samuel David grew up, the awareness of global events would shape his worldview. Discussions at school and within the community about social justice, human rights, and the importance of standing against oppression would likely have influenced his values and beliefs.

IN SUMMARY, AT SIX years old, Samuel David lived during a tumultuous time shaped by Stalin's terror, affecting Jewish communities worldwide. This period would have instilled a sense of resilience in him and an awareness of the broader struggles faced by Jews, influencing his life choices and community involvement in the years to come.

SAMUEL DAVID WAS JUST 15 years old when his mother, Leah, passed away in Kingston on July 28, 1941. This loss marked a significant turning point in his life.

Context of Leah's Death

1. Impact of Loss: Losing a parent during adolescence is a profound experience that can shape a young person's identity and outlook on life. Samuel would have faced not only the emotional turmoil of grief but also the responsibilities that might have fallen on him within the family structure.

---

2. CULTURAL AND FAMILIAL Expectations: As a Jewish boy, Samuel was likely expected to step up and support his family during this challenging time. The Jewish community often emphasizes the

importance of family, and after his mother's passing, he may have had to take on more responsibilities at home.

---

3. COMMUNITY SUPPORT: In Jewish tradition, the community plays a vital role in providing support during times of mourning. Samuel's family would have received condolences and assistance from friends, neighbors, and members of the Beth Israel synagogue, which could have helped alleviate some of the burdens during this difficult period.

LIFE AFTER LEAH'S DEATH

1. Emotional Growth: The loss of his mother may have led Samuel to mature quickly, learning to cope with grief and the realities of life without her guidance. It might have influenced his relationships with siblings and shaped his understanding of life and loss.

---

2. EDUCATION AND FUTURE Aspirations: Following his mother's death, Samuel may have channeled his emotions into his studies or hobbies, focusing on building a future for himself. His teenage years, marked by the impact of World War II, could have ignited a passion for social issues, community involvement, or perhaps even a desire to advocate for others facing similar hardships.

---

3. INFLUENCE ON RELATIONSHIPS: The experience of losing a parent often affects how young people form relationships in the future. Samuel may have become more empathetic and understanding,

fostering close bonds with friends and family as he sought connection and support.

---

4. RESILIENCE: THIS pivotal moment in Samuel's life likely contributed to developing resilience, a trait that would serve him well in the face of future challenges, including the impact of World War II and its aftermath.

CONCLUSION

Leah's passing in 1941 was a significant loss for Samuel David, shaping his character and influencing his path forward. As he navigated his teenage years, he carried the weight of grief while learning to find strength within himself and his community. This experience would undoubtedly leave a lasting impression on his life and contribute to his identity as he moved into adulthood.

SAMUEL DAVID WAS 23 years old when Canada became a founding member of NATO (North Atlantic Treaty Organization) on April 4, 1949. This was a significant period in history, reflecting both the geopolitical climate of the time and the emerging role of Canada on the world stage.

Context of Canada Joining NATO

1. Geopolitical Climate: The formation of NATO occurred in the aftermath of World War II, during a time when the threat of communism was rising, particularly with the Soviet Union's influence expanding across Eastern Europe. The alliance aimed to provide

collective defense against aggression and promote stability in Western nations.

---

2. CANADA'S ROLE: AS a founding member, Canada positioned itself as a key player in international relations. The country was moving away from its previous isolationist policies and recognizing the importance of collaboration with allies in the defense of democracy and freedom.

---

3. MILITARY PREPAREDNESS: Joining NATO meant that Canada committed to participating in military planning and ensuring its own defense capabilities. This period saw increased investments in the Canadian military, which would have implications for Samuel as he began to navigate adulthood in a world that was very much shaped by international conflict and alliances.

LIFE AFTER CANADA JOINED NATO

1. Career Opportunities: As a young man during this time, Samuel may have found new opportunities in various fields, including government, defense, and international relations, as Canada sought individuals to support its NATO commitments. The war had also impacted educational and job prospects, pushing many young people, including Samuel, to seek careers that would align with national priorities.

---

2. NATIONAL IDENTITY: The formation of NATO contributed to a sense of national identity for Canadians. Samuel and his peers may have felt a growing sense of pride and responsibility as they engaged

with the international community, understanding that Canada was playing a vital role in global peacekeeping and defense.

---

3. PERSONAL DEVELOPMENT: At 23, Samuel was likely at a crossroads in his life, where the realities of international relations could influence his thoughts on politics, security, and even personal aspirations. The events of this period may have encouraged him to become more politically aware and engaged with societal issues.

---

4. COMMUNITY AND SOCIAL Movements: This period also saw the emergence of various social movements and discussions around civil rights, gender equality, and anti-war sentiments, especially as the Cold War progressed. Samuel may have been influenced by these movements, shaping his views on social justice and community involvement.

CONCLUSION

At the age of 23, Samuel David witnessed Canada take a significant step into global affairs by becoming a founding member of NATO. This experience likely shaped his understanding of his country's role in the world and influenced his personal and professional development during a pivotal time in history. As he navigated adulthood, the implications of NATO membership would resonate through his life, impacting his worldview and engagement with the broader community.

SAMUEL DAVID WAS 34 years old when Canada's first Bill of Rights was passed on August 10, 1960. This legislation marked a significant advancement in the protection of individual freedoms and rights in Canada.

Context of the Canadian Bill of Rights

1. Historical Significance: The Canadian Bill of Rights was the first federal law in Canada to recognize and protect human rights and fundamental freedoms. It laid the groundwork for future rights legislation, including the Canadian Charter of Rights and Freedoms, which would come into effect in 1982.

---

2. POLITICAL CLIMATE: The passage of the Bill of Rights was influenced by a growing awareness of civil liberties and human rights issues during the 1950s and 1960s. This period was characterized by social movements advocating for equality, justice, and protection against discrimination based on race, gender, and religion.

---

3. GOVERNMENT AND SOCIETY: The Bill was championed by then-Prime Minister John Diefenbaker, who viewed it as a necessary step to ensure that all Canadians were afforded equal treatment under the law. Samuel, at the age of 34, would have been part of a generation witnessing this shift towards recognizing the importance of individual rights in the Canadian legal framework.

IMPLICATIONS FOR SAMUEL David and Society

1. Legal and Social Changes: The introduction of the Bill of Rights meant that Canadians could challenge laws and government actions

that violated their rights. For Samuel, this could have represented a newfound confidence in seeking justice and asserting his rights, both personally and as a member of the Jewish community.

---

2. CIVIC ENGAGEMENT: As a young adult during this transformative time, Samuel may have become more engaged in discussions around civil rights and social justice. The Bill of Rights provided a framework for advocacy and activism, encouraging individuals to participate in civic life and contribute to the protection of human rights.

---

3. PERSONAL REFLECTION: At 34, Samuel may have reflected on the implications of the Bill of Rights for his family and community. As a Jewish man in Canada, he might have been particularly aware of the historical struggles faced by minority communities and how this new legislation could provide a safeguard against discrimination.

---

4. IMPACT ON FUTURE Generations: The Bill of Rights laid the groundwork for a more rights-oriented society in Canada, influencing future legislation and public policy. Samuel's children and their peers would grow up in a context where individual rights were formally recognized and protected, shaping their expectations and experiences in Canadian society.

CONCLUSION

At 34 years old, Samuel David witnessed a landmark moment in Canadian history with the passage of the Bill of Rights. This event not only marked a significant evolution in the recognition of individual freedoms but also influenced the political and social landscape of Canada. As he navigated life during this time, Samuel likely felt empowered by the changes around him, participating in a society that was increasingly committed to ensuring justice and equality for all its citizens.

SAMUEL DAVID PASSED away at the age of 49 on January 30, 1975, in Kingston, Ontario. His death came during a period of significant social and political change in Canada and around the world.

Context of 1975

1. Political Climate: The mid-1970s were marked by shifts in Canadian politics, with the Liberal Party led by Pierre Elliott Trudeau in power. Trudeau's government was focused on national unity, social justice, and economic issues, aiming to address concerns such as inflation and unemployment.

2. SOCIAL MOVEMENTS: The 1970s were a time of increased activism and social movements. Issues surrounding women's rights, Indigenous rights, and environmentalism gained momentum. Samuel may have witnessed these changes and the growing awareness of social justice, particularly regarding minority rights.

3. ECONOMIC ENVIRONMENT: The Canadian economy faced challenges in the 1970s, including rising inflation and economic uncertainty. These economic conditions could have impacted Samuel and his family, influencing their day-to-day lives and future planning.

4. JEWISH COMMUNITY: In Kingston and across Canada, the Jewish community continued to navigate its identity and heritage. The legacy of World War II and the Holocaust remained significant for many Jewish Canadians, shaping their perspectives on community, identity, and advocacy.

LEGACY AND IMPACT

1. Family Influence: Samuel's passing at 49 meant that he left behind a legacy for his children and family. He would have been a significant figure in their lives, and his values and experiences likely influenced their upbringing and perspectives.

2. COMMUNITY ENGAGEMENT: As a member of the Jewish community and a participant in local affairs, Samuel's contributions may have had lasting effects on his community. His involvement in organizations and advocacy may have inspired others to engage in social issues.

3. REFLECTION ON RIGHTS and Freedoms: Samuel's life spanned a crucial period in Canadian history, including the introduction of the Bill of Rights and the ongoing dialogue about civil liberties. His experiences during this transformative time would have shaped his views on rights, justice, and community.

4. CULTURAL IMPACT: As a Jew in Canada, Samuel was part of a broader narrative of immigrant experiences, resilience, and community building. His life and legacy would contribute to the rich tapestry of Jewish history in Canada.

CONCLUSION

Samuel David's passing in 1975 marked the end of a life lived during a dynamic era of change in Canada and the world. His experiences and contributions would leave an indelible mark on his family, community, and the evolving narrative of Canadian society. His legacy would continue through the stories and values imparted to future generations, reflecting the broader struggles and triumphs of the time.

LEST WE FORGET

—————

VOLUNTEERS NEEDED[1]

—————

[1] https://www.wikitree.com/wiki/Kizell-4

[2] https://www.wikitree.com/wiki/Cramer-2596

[3] https://www.wikitree.com/wiki/Cowan-3599

[4] https://www.wikitree.com/wiki/Kizell-5

[5] https://www.wikitree.com/wiki/Langbort-1

[6] https://www.wikitree.com/wiki/Longbort-1

[7] https://www.wikitree.com/wiki/Longbort-2

[8] https://www.wikitree.com/wiki/Ludwin-7

[9] https://www.wikitree.com/wiki/Marcus-662

[10] https://www.wikitree.com/wiki/Urtick-1

[11] https://www.wikitree.com/wiki/Marcus-663

[12] https://www.wikitree.com/wiki/Marcus-664

---

1. https://billiongraves.com/cemetery/Beth-Israel-Cemetery/322910/volunteer

Don't miss out!

Visit the website below and you can sign up to receive emails whenever Angeline Gallant publishes a new book. There's no charge and no obligation.

https://books2read.com/r/B-A-QGSI-SDCEF

BOOKS 2 READ

Connecting independent readers to independent writers.

Also by Angeline Gallant

A Dragon's Diary
Dreaming of Dragons

Calling Her Heart
Whisper of the Heart
No Turning Back
Forsake Me Not
Hear My Cry

FORGET ME NOT
Victoria, Ontario's Babies 1894 - 1895

GENERATIONS OF THE VOLGA
A Family's Legacy

Guardian of the Heart
Fallen Petals

Keeper Of Secrets
A Lady's Secret

Kingston's Love Chronicles
Springtime Promises

Midnight's Awakening
Heart of the Storm
Walking Through The Storm
Walking Through The Storm
Heart of the Storm

Secrets of the Underworld
Deklan's Dragons

Tell My Story Collection
Tell My Story: Germany 1851
Tell My Story: England 1852
Whispers From The Garrison Church

The Dervock Legacy
Echoes of Dervock

The Grave Whisperer
Cataraqui United Church Cemetery
Wedding Bells in Kingston, Ontario, Canada 1923
St. Paul's Anglican Churchyard Kingston, Ontario, Canada A-B
St. Paul's Anglican Churchyard, Kingston, Ontario, Canada C - D
St. Paul's Anglican Churchyard, Kingston, Ontario, Canada G - H
St. Paul's Anglican Churchyard, Kingston, Ontario, Canada J - N
St. Paul's Anglican Churchyard, Kingston, Ontario, Canada O - R
St. Paul's Anglican Churchyard, Kingston, Ontario, Canada S - T
St. Paul's Anglican Churchyard, Kingston, Ontario T - Z
Small Graveyards & Burial Grounds: Kingston, Ontario, Canada
Cataraqui United Church Cemetery 1
Cataraqui United Church Cemetery 2
Cataraqui United Church Cemetary 3
Cataraqui United Church Cemetery 4
Cataraqui United Church Cemetery 5
Beth Israel Cemetery
Cataraqui United Church Cemetery 6
Beneath the Surface: Echoes from Beth Israel Cemetery
Grave Tales: Discovering the Lives of Beth Israel

The Timeless Veil
Eternal Devotion

The Wolf Whisperer Series
Journey of the Heart
Cry of a Warrior
Wolf Whisperer volumes 1 & 2

Endless White
The Wolf Whisperer volumes 1 & 2

Timeless
The Time Keeper's Sanctuary

Timeless Whispers of Dervock Saga
Secrets of Dervock

Standalone
Winds of Change vol 1-3

Watch for more at https://www.goodreads.com/author/show/
19703964.Angeline_Gallant.

About the Author

Angeline Gallant is a Geneology addict who loves to work on her family tree and help others with theirs. This passion for history plays a huge role in her books as well.

An Old Stock Canadian and a homeschooling mother living in Canada, Angeline is determined to leave her own special mark on the world through her work, her child, and her writing.

Angeline is an author on Goodreads. If you follow her account on Goodreads, she will follow back.

Read more at https://www.goodreads.com/author/show/19703964.Angeline_Gallant.

www.ingramcontent.com/pod-product-compliance
Lightning Source LLC
Chambersburg PA
CBHW071521150726
48000CB00002B/633